Revise for OCR GCSE Textiles Technology

Carey Clarkson and Maria James

RECOGNISING ACHIEVEMENT

Heinemann Educational Publishers
Halley Court, Jordan Hill, Oxford OX2 8EJ
Part of Harcourt Education

Heinemann is the registered trademark of
Harcourt Education Limited

First published 2003

07 06 05 04 03 02
10 9 8 7 6 5 4 3 2 1

British Library Cataloguing in Publication Data is available
from the British Library on request.

ISBN 0 435 41714 2

Typeset by Tech-Set Ltd

Original illustrations © Harcourt Education Limited 2003

Illustrated by Tech-Set Ltd

Printed in the UK by The Bath Press Ltd, Bath.

Acknowledgements
The authors wish to thank Alexander Kaey and Nancy Clarkson.
Every effort has been made to contact copyright holders of material
reproduced in this book. Any omissions will be rectified in subsequent
printings if notice is given to the publishers.

Tel: 01865 888058 email: info.he@heinemann.co.uk

Contents

How to use this book

This book has been written as a revision guide for students studying the OCR specification for GCSE in Design and Technology (D&T): Textiles Technology. It can be used in conjunction with the following OCR resources:

- GCSE Textiles Technology for OCR student book, which gives more detailed information and coverage of the specification content
- OCR GCSE Design and Technology (D&T): Textile Technology specification.

The revision guide covers the content and guidance notes included in the specification. It contains a breakdown of the basic information and knowledge required to ensure that you are better prepared to answer any question set on any aspect of the specification content.

It is also advisable to keep yourself up-to-date with current developments in the relevant technologies, processes and materials by investigating a range of resources from the Internet to the local newspapers.

How this book is set out

The book is clearly set out with the following sections:

Specification reference points

The panel at the beginning of each section contains a list of the main points covered, reflecting the content and order in the specification.

Key words

The key words related to a particular section appear in panels in the margins and help you focus on and remember the important terms.

Key points

These summaries of the most important points in the section are useful as a quick revision resource.

Questions

The questions at the end of each section can be answered using the information in that section. To practice for the examination you can either:

- revisit the text to answer the questions
- answer the questions first and then use the text to check your understanding.

Activities

The activities at the end of each section will help you:

- practice applying the knowledge you have gathered from the section
- use strategies to re-structure the information and remember it more easily.

In some sections you will also see addresses of useful websites which you can visit for more information or revision guidance.

Exam guidance

The GCSE Design and Technology (D&T): Textiles Technology written examination allows you to demonstrate your specialist knowledge, skills and understanding of textiles technology by answering questions on the subject content outlined in the specification.

Question paper requirements

The combination of question papers you will take for the OCR GCSE in Textiles Technology depends on the tier of entry you are working on and whether you are taking the full or the short course.

Tier of entry

Papers 1 and 3 – Foundation tier papers, which allows you to achieve Grades G–C. They are both one hour long.

Papers 2 and 4 – Higher tier papers, which allows you to achieve Grades D–A*. They are both one hour and fifteen minutes long.

Full or short course

Full course students complete both question papers for their tier of entry.

Short course students complete only one question paper from either the foundation or higher tier of entry.

Papers 1 and 2 will include a product analysis question based on information contained in the question paper. The focus of this question will be on a different theme to the one in papers 3 and 4.

Papers 3 and 4 will also contain a product analysis question but on a theme published before the examination. The theme can be researched in advance, but information gathered **cannot** be taken into the examination.

Structure of the question papers

There are five compulsory questions on each paper and each question is worth ten marks. The questions are divided into sub-sections. The easier questions are at the beginning and they become gradually more difficult towards the end of the paper. The harder questions require more detailed answers, showing more technical knowledge.

Examination technique

A typical question is given below. Lots of tips have been added to help you answer similar questions successfully.

1 The manufacturer of high-visibility vests wishes to extend the range to include a fashion Gilet/waistcoat as shown below.

a The prototype Gilet/waistcoat is to be made.
   Name a suitable fabric for the prototype.

.... (1)

b Consumer preference shows that current teenage fashion items use linen.
   Give **one** reason why linen has become popular for teenage fashion items.

.... (1)

c Linen-based materials are expensive in comparison to alternatives.
   Explain how CAD/CAM could be used by the manufacturer to reduce wastage.

....

....

.... (3)

Top tips

- Time available to answer each question: as a guide, 12 minutes for foundation tier and 15 minutes for higher tier.

- Words such as 'list', 'state' or 'name' usually indicate that one-word answers are acceptable.

- Words such as 'describe' and 'analyse' usually require a more detailed, structured answer.

- If asked to draw a diagram, you should draw one. Add clear annotation (labels) where required.

- If you are asked to design or draw an item, look at the number of marks allocated for it and include at least that number of features in the design. Some indication of colour will be expected in design questions.

- The marks allocated for each part of the question are a good guide to the amount of detail needed in the answer.

- The amount of space (number of lines) is another clue to how detailed the answer should be.

- A product analysis question will always ask you to apply your knowledge to the wider effects of design and technology on society and industrial practice, as well as to show your understanding of the design and make process.

- Spelling is not crucial, but legible handwriting is. Marks are not lost if a word is spelt incorrectly, but they are if the examiner cannot read and understand your answer.

- Remember to use the knowledge you have gained from your internal assessment (coursework) piece. Questions often refer to the design and make process you have actively experienced.

Summary

You need to be thoroughly prepared for the examinations as they are worth 40% of your final mark. This means that the recommended time allowance for examination preparation is 26 hours.

Have fun!

Designing and Making

Developing and writing a design brief

This section will cover:

- Using different information sources to identify design problems and the design need.
- Identifying users and the intended market of the product.
- Developing a design brief for a marketable product.

Using information sources to identify design problems and the design need

Different **information sources** can be used as starting points to research your task. To find the information needed to identify design problems and a design need you can use a variety of sources.

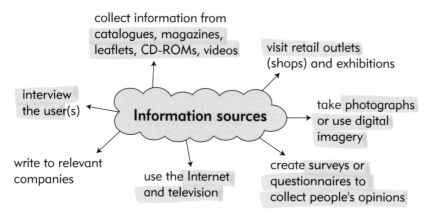

collect information from catalogues, magazines, leaflets, CD-ROMs, videos

visit retail outlets (shops) and exhibitions

interview the user(s)

Information sources

take photographs or use digital imagery

write to relevant companies

use the Internet and television

create surveys or questionnaires to collect people's opinions

Identifying users and the intended market for the product

It is important to be able to identify the **users** and the **intended market** for a product if it is to truly satisfy a need. For example, most teenagers like their bedrooms to be comfortable and fashionable and are therefore more likely to buy a product that fulfils both of these requirements.

Developing a design brief for a marketable product

The task

> 'Toys help children to learn. Design and make a prototype toy that would help in the development of an identified skill (or skills) of a pre-school child.'

After suitable research into the intended market and user, the **design brief** might be:

> 'Toys help children to learn. I will design and make a prototype toy that will help in the development of hand–eye co-ordination of a 3-year-old child and will be sold through the Early Learning Centre.'

Key words

Information sources include text, drawings, photographs, graphics and media clippings.

The **user** is the person or people who will use the product, which is designed to take account of their needs.

The **intended market** for a product is the range of potential users or the group of people who the designer considers will use or buy the product.

A **design brief** is a short, clear statement outlining the design problem. It should contain the words 'design and make' and be linked to the original task.

Key points

- You should be able to identify design problems and the design need from a number of information sources.
- The user and the intended market for a product should always be considered if the finished product is to truly satisfy the need.
- A design brief is a short, clear statement outlining the design problem.

Activities

1 Look at the task below – who is the intended user for the toy?

2 Now look at the design brief above – who is the intended user for the toy?

3 Complete the mind map below to show how the design brief might be developed. The reasoning behind the selection of the age group has already been filled in for you.

Age of the child must be considered. Pre-school covers 0–5 years.
This could be broken down for research into:

- 0–18 months
- 18 months–3 years
- 3–4 years
- 4–5 years

Task: Toys help children to learn. Design and make a prototype toy that would help in the development of an identified skill (or skills) of a pre-school child

Drawing up a specification

This section will cover:

- Examining the purpose of the product
- Identifying and collecting data
- Considering planning
- Identifying and evaluating existing products
- Considering manufacture in batches
- Drawing up a written specification.

Examining the purpose of the product

It is important at the beginning of the design process to understand the intended **purpose**, form and function of the product to be made.

It can be helpful to do the following.

1 Look at how similar or the same product was used in the past and compare these findings with how the product is used now. For example, swimwear worn in the early 1900s reflected a fashion trend within society. Swimwear today also reflects fashion trends.

2 Break down the purpose of the product into the following sub-headings.

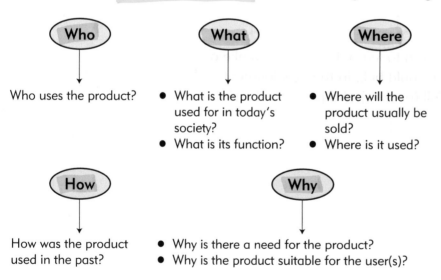

Who

Who uses the product?

What

- What is the product used for in today's society?
- What is its function?

Where

- Where will the product usually be sold?
- Where is it used?

How

How was the product used in the past?

Why

- Why is there a need for the product?
- Why is the product suitable for the user(s)?

These five sub-headings can stimulate further questions and research into the design brief from which conclusions for the design specification can be drawn.

Identifying and collecting data

It is important to identify and collect relevant data. For example, designs for a child's toy should consider safety regulations. The following are the most common sources of data that you will need to consider.

Key word

The **purpose** is the reason for a product. For example, a child's winter hat protects the head and retains the heat, providing warmth.

The British Standards Institute (BSI)

[handwritten: checks safety of products being sold to the general public to a british standards]

This organisation provides 'rules, guidelines and characteristics' to be used in designing and making products. Many British standards have now merged with European standards. For example, the British Standard for Toys is known as BSEN71, which merges both the British (BS) and the European (EN) standard.

BSI registered Firm Symbol

The International Organisation for Standardisation (ISO)

[handwritten: Promotes the development of Standardisation]

This world-wide federation promotes the development of standardisation and related activities in the world of designing and making.

ISO symbol

CE Marking

[handwritten: meets the requirements of all the relevant European Union directives and can be sold legally.]

The CE symbol, which comes from the French phrase 'Conformité Européene', indicates that a product meets the requirements of all the relevant European Union directives and can be legally sold within the European Union.

CE symbol

Useful websites

Please go to www.heinemann.co.uk/hotlinks and enter the code 7142P

Anthropometric data

These data give detailed dimensions or measurements of the human body. For example, the variation in the length of leg measurements of children of different ages and how this impacts on the range of sizes used for a style of trouser.

Considering planning

There are two most important issues that affect planning.

Environmental issues

Consideration of the effects the product being designed will have on the environment in terms of:

- selection of resources for manufacture (**renewable** or **non-renewable**)
- pollution implications
- disposal at the end of the recyclable or biodegradable products' useful life (see pages 29 and 90 for further information on recycling).

Key words

Renewable resources are those found naturally in nature, or living things which can be re-grown and used again. Examples of these types of resources are fibres and fabrics made from sustainable crops such as cotton and linen.

Non-renewable resources are those in limited supply. Examples of these type of resources are skins from animals and silk fibres from the cultivated silkworm.

Cost issues

Consideration of the costs involved in the manufacture of the product. The materials and components used and the production methods will have a big impact upon the final cost.

Identifying and evaluating existing products

To find out how successfully a product fulfils a need, it is useful to identify, analyse and evaluate an **existing product**.

To do this you need to take into account the needs of the intended user(s). Consider the following perspectives:

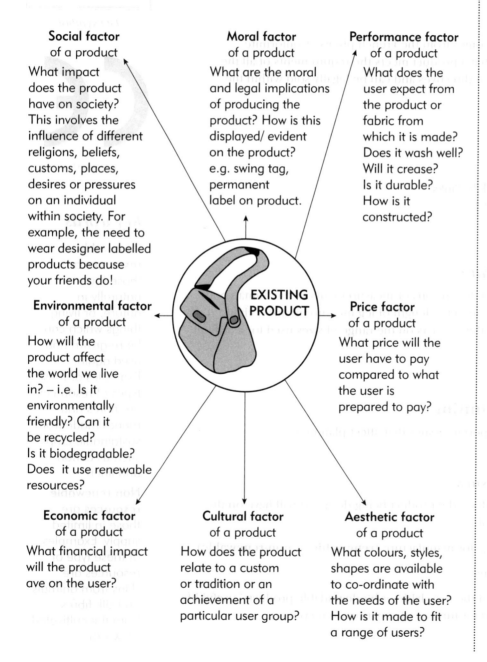

Social factor
of a product

What impact does the product have on society? This involves the influence of different religions, beliefs, customs, places, desires or pressures on an individual within society. For example, the need to wear designer labelled products because your friends do!

Moral factor
of a product

What are the moral and legal implications of producing the product? How is this displayed/ evident on the product? e.g. swing tag, permanent label on product.

Performance factor
of a product

What does the user expect from the product or fabric from which it is made? Does it wash well? Will it crease? Is it durable? How is it constructed?

Environmental factor
of a product

How will the product affect the world we live in? – i.e. Is it environmentally friendly? Can it be recycled? Is it biodegradable? Does it use renewable resources?

EXISTING PRODUCT

Price factor
of a product

What price will the user have to pay compared to what the user is prepared to pay?

Economic factor
of a product

What financial impact will the product ave on the user?

Cultural factor
of a product

How does the product relate to a custom or tradition or an achievement of a particular user group?

Aesthetic factor
of a product

What colours, styles, shapes are available to co-ordinate with the needs of the user? How is it made to fit a range of users?

Considering manufacture in batches

Consideration of how the product is to be produced in a batch quantity is important. Commercial production systems are explained fully on page 22.

Drawing up a written specification

A **design specification** shows how the product is expected to function when in use and draws together all your research points. It usually includes the following points:

Design specification

- Time-scale of production.

- Function of the product.

- Performance – how and where is the product meant to work?

- Aesthetics and appearance of the product.

- Materials – suitable to use for the product?

- Important performance characteristics.

- Manufacture and quantity – how will the product eventually be

  commercially produced?

- Cost – do you have a budget?

- Size – anthropometrics and specific dimensions to be considered.

- Target market – which group of people are you designing for?

- Ergonomics – how does the product interact with the user?

- Life in service – how long will the product be expected to last?

- Weight – does it matter if the product is light or heavy?

- Safety – what safety factors and regulations need to be

  considered?

- Environmental issues – are there any environmental

  requirements?

- Quality – how will you produce a martketable product?

- Storage.

Key points

At the beginning of a design activity it is important to understand the purpose of the product to be designed.

- You should be able to collect data that is relevant to the design of the product.

- Market research is the gathering of information about products by asking people's opinions and seeing what is already available.

- You should consider how existing products fulfil the needs of intended users by examining them from moral, social, economic, environmental and cultural perspectives.

- A specification should consider the feasibility to manufacture in batches.

- A specification is a list of the key points a design must have or do.

Activities

1 Take an existing product, such as a mobile phone case, and research data that is relevant to the design of the product. Use the website addresses at www.heinemann.co.uk/hotlinks to help you. Present your findings as a mind map.

2 Write out a clear design specification for your chosen product.

3 Use your specification points to produce a presentation to promote the product to a partner. You are only allowed to use ten actual words within your promotional presentation so you must think of other ways to explain the merits of your product.

Generating design proposals

It is important to understand the nature of design work and how your knowledge could be tested in the examination. The following information provides a knowledge base that you will need to apply to any examination question on designing textile items.

Generating a range of design proposals

Designers need to consider a range of design proposals for any one product to meet the identified needs of the user(s). The following stages are involved in the design of a textile product before manufacturing.

1 **Mood boards** to act as a starting point for an idea.
2 Initial ideas or **thumbnail sketches**, which experiment with elements such as styles, shapes and patterns.
3 **Working drawings** to show a detailed outline of the product and include:

- the material(s) to be used
- the shape
- the size
- possible trim details

- fastening ideas
- **embellishment** ideas
- construction methods.

Working drawings require clear and detailed **annotations** to show how the design meets the need of the design specification.

Evaluating design ideas

When evaluating design ideas it is useful to cover the points already discussed and also consider those shown below:

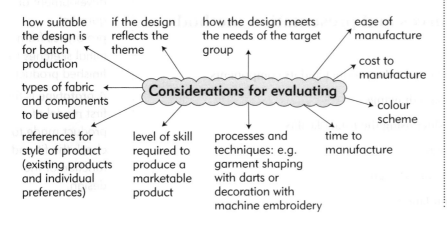

how suitable the design is for batch production

if the design reflects the theme

how the design meets the needs of the target group

ease of manufacture

types of fabric and components to be used

Considerations for evaluating

cost to manufacture

colour scheme

references for style of product (existing products and individual preferences)

level of skill required to produce a marketable product

processes and techniques: e.g. garment shaping with darts or decoration with machine embroidery

time to manufacture

At this stage a product may be modified if necessary. In industry, the use of CAD allows designers to view all sides of the design and enables modification of the product on screen if necessary.

Understanding the relevance of function and aesthetics

Designers must strike a balance between the appearance of a design (aesthetics) and the demands of what it has to do (function).

Using mood boards

In industry mood boards not only act as a starting point for a design, but can also be used to check the feasibility of a design idea. This can be done by testing:

- the yarns identified on the design and by creating swatches of fabric using different structures

- how the yarns look, feel and handle

- the suitability of the design features and construction techniques, for example, a pocket style.

All these findings can be sketched and added to the mood board to present to the client or manufacturer for approval.

Considering the reasons for selecting a design proposal

From the range of working drawings, a final design proposal needs to be identified. The reasons for selection need to be clearly evident through:

- clear annotations examining construction details, manufacturing in quantity, aesthetic and functional qualities, and design features

- reference to current trends in fashion, colour, cost, quality, consumer groups, fibres and components.

Identifying resources and presentation methods

CAD software is used to:

- produce accurate drawings of the product and its components

- produce 2D or 3D design drawings

- view all sides of a product using the rotate facility

- enlarge parts of a design

- amend or modify parts of a design

- carry out tests and simulations.

Key word

Computer-aided design (CAD) helps in the development of garment prototypes from initial sketches to finished product.

A **prototype** is the first model of a product made to check the fit and function of the design.

It is important that you understand how ICT (information communications technology) can be used to enhance your design work.

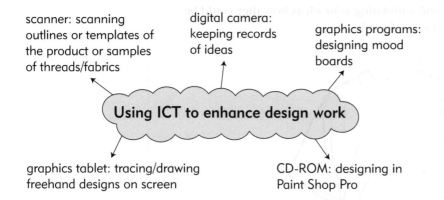

scanner: scanning outlines or templates of the product or samples of threads/fabrics

digital camera: keeping records of ideas

graphics programs: designing mood boards

Using ICT to enhance design work

graphics tablet: tracing/drawing freehand designs on screen

CD-ROM: designing in Paint Shop Pro

Key points

- You can design a product using mood boards, thumbnail sketches, working drawings, a final design proposal, CAD and a prototype.
- A thumbnail sketch is a quick, basic freehand sketch of an idea.
- A working drawing is a detailed drawing of a design proposal.
- A final design is a completed, fully annotated design idea which is evaluated against the original specification.
- A mood board can act as a starting point for an idea and as a check on feasibility.
- CAD means computer-aided design.

In the examination you may have to use your knowledge in a variety of ways, such as:

- to create a product specification from a design idea
- to explain how a design meets the points in the specification
- to explain the meaning of specific terms within the design process
- to re-design an existing product.

Activities

1 Produce a range of thumbnail sketches, with a theme of 'Time', for a mobile phone cover . You must present your ideas in black and white only and cover just one side of A4 paper.

2 Produce a working drawing of one of your ideas.

3 Evaluate your final idea by clearly listing the main specification points.

4 List three other ways you could enhance your final design with the use of ICT.

Question

The pictures below show initial designs for a staff uniform for a leisure centre. Show by sketching and annotating your ideas how they could be developed to project a corporate identity.

Product development

This section will cover:

- Testing and trialling
- Matching materials with tools, equipment and processes
- Developing a system of control for individual and batch production
- Using ICT to present the final design proposal.

Product development is about making decisions as to which materials, pre-manufactured components and production processes to use to make the proposed design.

Testing and trialling

The main aim of testing and trialling is to make decisions about the materials, components and processes to use in order to improve the quality of the product for the user.

Materials

Every type of fibre has different **performance characteristics** and it is important to know what these are so that the best one can be chosen for a product.

durability – in relation to wear and tear or colour

abrasion and pilling – in relation to wear and rubbing

absorbency – how easily water or other liquids are absorbed

insulation – prevention of heat loss

tensile strength – how strong

Criteria for testing performance of fabrics and fibres

stretch and recovery – how well it stretches and returns to original size and shape

flammability – how flammable

water proofness – how resistant to water

wind proofness – how permeable

fading – how colourfast

drape – how well it 'falls' as a fabric

aftercare – washing, ironing and stain removal: response to temperature change, vigorous washing and chemicals

Pre-manufactured components

Some parts of the design are specially made and others bought as standard pre-manufactured components. There is little point in making parts that can be purchased at a reasonable cost. For example, a cross-way strip binding could be made or a ready-made bias binding could be bought in. To test and trial pre-manufactured components you need to compare the existing components, for example, you might compare the use of a polyester thread and a silk thread for stitching Elastane.

Production processes

During the design and make stages of a product, questions are asked to determine the most appropriate production processes to use, taking into account the performance characteristics of the materials and the quantity of the product to be made. Use the information on industrial applications on pages 51–56 to develop your understanding further.

Optimum sizes

The most suitable or optimum size for the product must also be decided. This is often tested with the use of a **toile**, which is made up to test different style ideas, drape and fit as well as size. Toiles or prototypes, with surveys, questionnaires and one-to-one discussion, are also used to test sales appeal. Styles that lack appeal are either eliminated or have their design features changed to meet the needs of the user(s).

Matching materials with tools, equipment and processes

It is important to match materials and other components with suitable tools, equipment and processes when deciding how to manufacture the product in quantity. For example, a computer controlled embroidery machine will produce a better quality finish in less time than it takes to sew the same design by hand. These decisions are formed by considering the following factors (see also the information on tools and equipment on pages 31–33):

- costs and availability of suitable materials and components
- production costs
- time-scale for production

Developing a system of control for individual and batch production

Appropriate use of commercial **paper patterns** and templates can be used to simulate commercial production and ensure that a quality product of the same size can be made over and over again.

Commercial patterns

These can be bought from shops and consist of three main parts:

- pattern pieces made of thin, tissue-like paper
- instruction sheet
- envelope

It is very important to know what pattern pieces look like and what the symbols mean. Study the diagram below carefully.

Key word

A **toile** is a fabric version of a pattern, which can be modified to get the desired look and fit.

Key word

A **paper pattern** is a way to produce complex shapes, allowing fabric to be cut accurately.

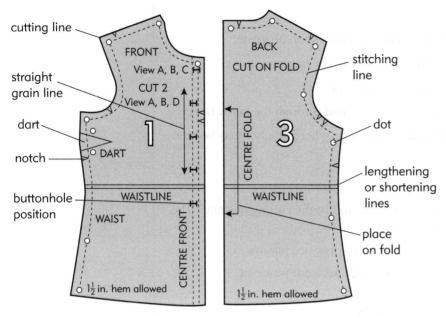

Symbols used on patterns

Making and grading patterns

Patterns for garments are made from basic blocks in standard body sizes in the following stages:

1   A basic block is made for each piece of the garment, such as the bodice and sleeve sections.

2   The blocks for the pattern may be adapted on a computer if the design is changed.

3   Then the pattern pieces are graded to fit larger and smaller sizes. This can be done by computer program which calculates and adds the scale of **grading** to the pattern pieces. You can see the grading on a multi-size commercial pattern.

4   The pattern pieces are placed on the fabric as a pattern lay, following the instruction sheet and the symbols on the pattern.

Pattern lay

A pattern lay is the optimum layout of the pattern pieces on the fabric, placing them as close together as possible to reduce waste and cost. In a fully automated system the pieces can be moved around on screen until the optimum layout is achieved. The finished pattern lay can also be stored or printed out. A complete pattern lay for the product can then be sent directly to the cutting machine.

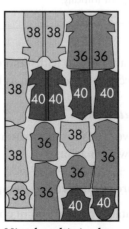

Mixed multi-size lay with different shades showing different sizes

Key word

Grading is the process of making adjustments to the pattern pieces to make it fit larger and smaller sizes.

23

Marking

There are various ways in which notches and marks can be made.

- **Drill markers** – make a small visible hole in the fabric.
- **Dye markers** – holes are marked by a colour.
- **Thread markers** – a tacking thread is stitched through the fabric layers.
- A **hot notcher** – marks the edge of the fabric where notches may be seen on the pattern pieces.

Cutting

Instructions are sent directly from the computer to the cutting machine. The fabric is cut using one of the following:

- knife or scissors
- laser beam
- high pressure plasma
- high pressure water jet.

Circular cutters, scissors, straight knife and band knife
- all processes done by hand
- slow production processes
- process reliant on the skill of the operator.

Die cutter
- pattern pieces are stamped out to give identical shapes
- expensive to make.

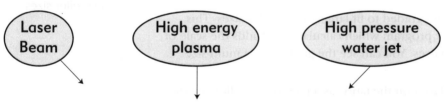

- all are fully automated, accurate, fast and economical
- expensive to install equipment initially.

The sewing process

Industrial sewing machines are built to withstand continuous operation at high sewing speeds. They are therefore known as high speed machines.

Automated sewing machines

It is useful to know about two types for the written examination: profile sewing systems and CNC sewing machines.

Profile sewing systems – are controlled by a template and a jig. They:

- allow accurate and repeatable production of components, for example pocket flaps
- produce items of a consistent quality.

CNC sewing machines – are controlled by computer using one of two modes:

- learning mode – the operator takes the machine manually through each step of the sewing
- the process and the information is then stored for future production runs
- off-line programming – the sewing cycle is digitised and stored.

Quality is monitored continuously through the computer to identify and rectify faults without holding up production. These types of machines are fast, efficient, effective, flexible enough to cope with a variety of tasks and needs, and allow production at a reasonable cost.

Key word

CNC means computerised numerical control.

Using ICT to present the final design proposal

You need to know how ICT is used in the development of a product. The main ways ICT can be used are to:

- generate ideas
- develop and model ideas
- communicate product tests.

In industry computer-aided design (CAD) and computer-aided manufacture (CAM) are used extensively in the product development process.

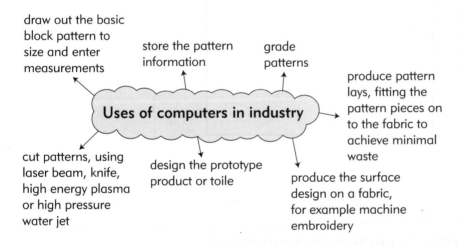

In the classroom a variety of ICT equipment can be used to record testing and trialling.

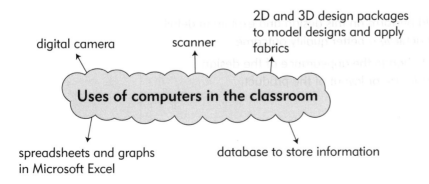

Key points

The key elements of product development are:

- testing and trialling
- matching materials with tools, equipment and process
- developing a system to control manufacture individually and in quantity
- using ICT to generate, develop, model and communicate design proposals.

Question

Complete the table below by finding out the meaning of each symbol. Record your answer in a way you find easy to remember.

Pattern Symbol	Meaning (explanation in use)
←————→	=
○- - - - - -○	=
▽	=
↑___↑	=
(zigzag line)	=
═══	=
●	=

Activities

1 Select a commercial pattern. Discuss the testing and trialling that might have taken place before the pattern reached its point of sale.

2 Look at the design of the garment on the pattern envelope you have selected.

   a List five tests you would perform on this design and explain in detail how these tests would achieve a better quality outcome.

   b Discuss how you might change the appearance of the design without altering the basic size or layout of the product.

Product planning

Producing a detailed plan of work

It is important to produce a detailed plan of work with realistic time schedules both for your own coursework and in industry. A plan of work should include details of a number of elements.

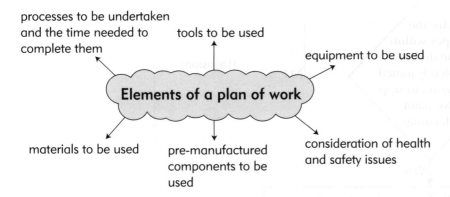

The presentation of the plan of work can take on many different formats. The most popular are shown below.

Flow charts

A flow chart is a diagrammatic way of showing an order of work using the standard symbols shown below.

Arrows indicate the direction of flow of the tasks and may show flow in the opposite direction if a stage has to be repeated. Look carefully at the diagram because it is important that you know what these symbols mean and how they are used in planning for your written examination.

Example flowchart for a silk scarf

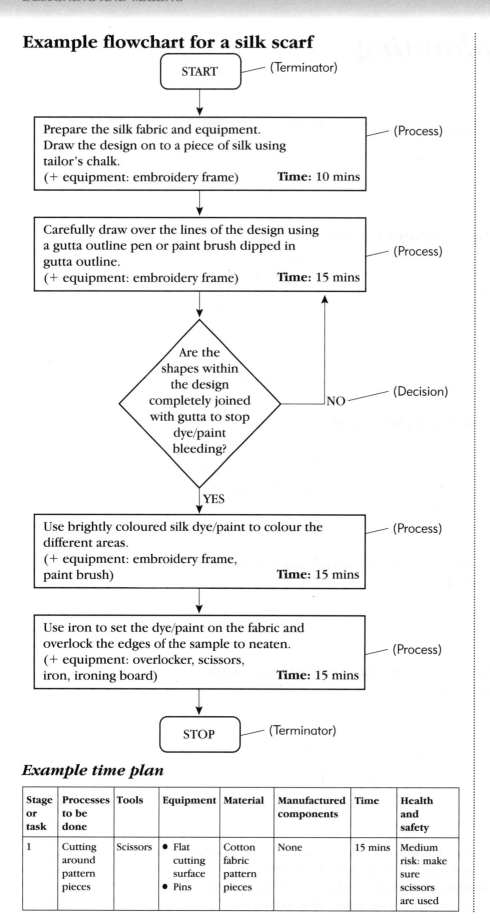

START — (Terminator)

Prepare the silk fabric and equipment.
Draw the design on to a piece of silk using
tailor's chalk.
(+ equipment: embroidery frame)   **Time:** 10 mins   — (Process)

Carefully draw over the lines of the design using
a gutta outline pen or paint brush dipped in
gutta outline.
(+ equipment: embroidery frame)   **Time:** 15 mins   — (Process)

Are the shapes within the design completely joined with gutta to stop dye/paint bleeding? — NO — (Decision)

YES

Use brightly coloured silk dye/paint to colour the
different areas.
(+ equipment: embroidery frame,
paint brush)   **Time:** 15 mins   — (Process)

Use iron to set the dye/paint on the fabric and
overlock the edges of the sample to neaten.
(+ equipment: overlocker, scissors,
iron, ironing board)   **Time:** 15 mins   — (Process)

STOP — (Terminator)

Example time plan

Stage or task	Processes to be done	Tools	Equipment	Material	Manufactured components	Time	Health and safety
1	Cutting around pattern pieces	Scissors	• Flat cutting surface • Pins	Cotton fabric pattern pieces	None	15 mins	Medium risk: make sure scissors are used

Industrial time plans can be presented in chart format as above. They take into account the following considerations:

- start and finish times or dates
- preparation and clearing away time
- availability of tools and equipment
- quality control checks
- unforeseen problems
- absence through illness
- breakdown in machinery
- unavailability of materials and components
- health and safety.

Preparing materials economically

It is important to prepare materials economically and to use pre-manufactured components appropriately if a product is to be cost-effective. Unnecessary waste will make a product more expensive because all the materials have to be paid for. The creation of waste also raises environmental and recycling issues, which are discussed on page 90.

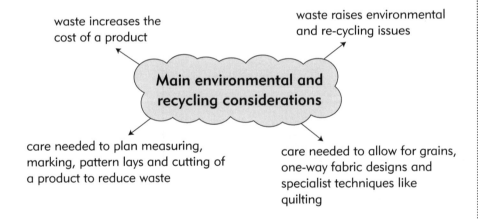

waste increases the cost of a product

waste raises environmental and re-cycling issues

Main environmental and recycling considerations

care needed to plan measuring, marking, pattern lays and cutting of a product to reduce waste

care needed to allow for grains, one-way fabric designs and specialist techniques like quilting

Quilting – the stitching of three layers of fabric together causes the pieces to shrink in size: the finished piece of quilting is smaller than the pre-quilted fabric. To avoid waste:

- quilt the fabric before cutting out the pattern pieces *or*
- cut out the fabric to a size to allow for quilting and then quilt the individual pieces.

One-way fabric designs – also need careful consideration. Fabric that is striped or checked needs to be cut out so that the design matches when the pieces are sewn together. This normally requires more fabric because the pattern pieces have to be moved to a suitable position in relation to the fabric design, which in turn leads to higher costs.

Fabrics with a grain, nap or pile – like velvet and corduroy also have to be considered in the same way.

Key points

- Planning must include all the materials and pre-manufactured components needed as well as the tools and equipment
- It is important to prepare materials economically and use pre-manufactured components appropriately in order to avoid waste.

Activity

Take any item you have made and produce a detailed flow chart or time plan of work. Make sure you include the key items that have been listed in this section.

Tools and equipment

This section will cover:

- Selecting tools and equipment and using them safely
- Using coloured media
- Using tools and equipment for making
- Using joining tools and equipment
- Using finishing tools and equipment
- Considering presentation for marketing and labelling.
- Using cutting tools

Selecting tools and equipment and using them safely

You will need to know how to use the range of tools and equipment in the following sections. You will also need to match industrial tools and equipment for the relevant processes and show an understanding of safe working practice. When using any tools or equipment it is important to be able to use them effectively and safely. Safe working practice for both personal safety and for the safety of others must be addressed.

Using colouring media

Different colouring media can be used to enhance drawings and to show details of colour and pattern. Equipment to use can be:

- black pen to highlight important details
- coloured pens and pencils to highlight and to create effects such as 3D to your drawings.

Using tools and equipment for making

When designing and making textile items, a wide variety of tools and equipment needs to be used. Knowledge about all of them is necessary not only to produce a high quality product, but also to ensure safe working practice.

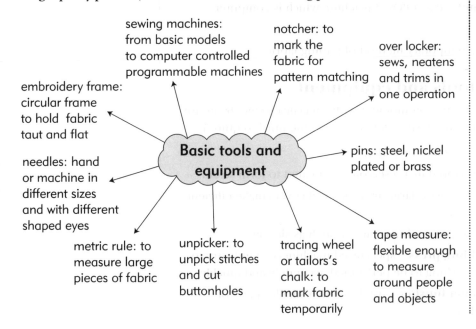

sewing machines: from basic models to computer controlled programmable machines

notcher: to mark the fabric for pattern matching

over locker: sews, neatens and trims in one operation

embroidery frame: circular frame to hold fabric taut and flat

needles: hand or machine in different sizes and with different shaped eyes

Basic tools and equipment

pins: steel, nickel plated or brass

metric rule: to measure large pieces of fabric

unpicker: to unpick stitches and cut buttonholes

tracing wheel or tailors's chalk: to mark fabric temporarily

tape measure: flexible enough to measure around people and objects

31

Using cutting tools

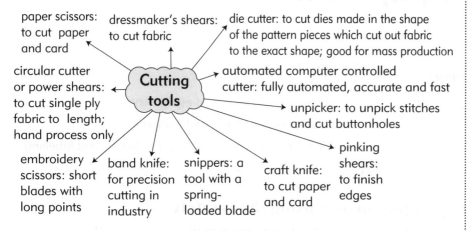

paper scissors: to cut paper and card

dressmaker's shears: to cut fabric

die cutter: to cut dies made in the shape of the pattern pieces which cut out fabric to the exact shape; good for mass production

circular cutter or power shears: to cut single ply fabric to length; hand process only

Cutting tools

automated computer controlled cutter: fully automated, accurate and fast

unpicker: to unpick stitches and cut buttonholes

embroidery scissors: short blades with long points

band knife: for precision cutting in industry

snippers: a tool with a spring-loaded blade

craft knife: to cut paper and card

pinking shears: to finish edges

Using joining tools and equipment

You will need to be able to identify and list tools and equipment that can be used for both permanent and temporary joining. Each piece of equipment has advantages and disadvantages, most items of large equipment are electrically operated and many are computer controlled.

- **Sewing machines** – include basic, automatic and computer controlled machines. Each model varies, some allowing the user to design their own stitches, others supplying computer disks to increase the number of stitch options. All give a method of permanent joining.

- **Over lockers** – have no bobbin and use three or four cones of thread from the top. The machine stitches the seam, neatens the edge and trims away the excess fabric in one operation, thus speeding up these processes. The result is a permanent join.

- **Knitting machines** – can be computer controlled with programmable software and result in permanent joining.

- **Embroidery machines** – e.g. a POEM machine which is computer controlled.

- **Pins and needles** – a temporary method of joining fabric.

Using finishing tools and equipment

Finishing can involve a variety of equipment with specialist usage. Irons are used for pressing and can vary in style depending on the finish required.

- **Dry iron** – using just heat and pressure.

- **Steam iron** – water is stored in a reservoir and heated to form steam.

- **Ironing board** – used to press large areas; special covers make efficient use of heat from the iron.

- **Sleeve board** – used to press tubular pieces, such as sleeves.

- **Flat press and moulding press** – specialised machinery in industry to enable pressing and finishing to be performed accurately and quickly.

- **Steam dolly and tunnel finisher** – used to finish smaller parts of garments, such as collars.

Considering presentation for marketing and labelling

Finished textile products are packaged for transportation and sometimes for presentation to the consumer. Packaging is used to enhance the product and to provide information to the user. Labelling tells the consumer key facts about the product, such as:

- a brief description of the product
- fibre content and trade or brand names
- aftercare symbols
- quality marks showing how the product conforms to particular standards.

Key points

- You should be able to use a range of tools, equipment and processes for making, cutting, joining and finishing effectively and safely.
- Remember that in the examination, marks are only awarded for the full and correct names of tools and equipment.

Activities

1 List all the tools and equipment you used in objective five of your textiles coursework project. Explain why each piece was chosen.

2 Compare your list of tools and equipment with those that would have been used if your product was going to be commercially manufactured.

3 Draw a label to be fitted into a garment with all the relevant information for a consumer.

Processes

This section will cover:

- Joining fabrics
- Using aesthetic and creative techniques
- Using functional finishes.

Joining Fabrics

There are temporary and permanent ways to join a fabric.

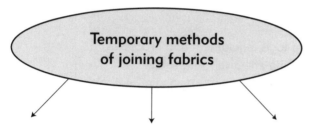

Fastenings
- can be used to allow sections to be temporarily joined while the product is being made
- examples include Velcro, zips, buttons and buttonholes.

Tacking
- stitches usually done by hand, but can also be done using a machine
- approximately 1 cm long and are removed once the fabric is permanently joined.

Pins
- used to hold fabric together before permanently joining.

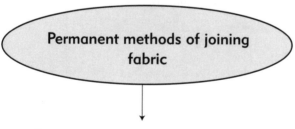

Seams
- sewing two pieces of fabric together.

Seams

There is a range of different types of seams and it is important to have an understanding of how each one is made and be able to recognise each one visually to make the appropriate choice.

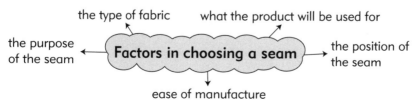

It is important to remember that the stitching line for a seam on commercial patterns is usually 1.5 cm from the edge of the fabric. This is known as the **seam allowance**. In industry, the seam allowance can be smaller than 1.5 cm to save fabric and therefore costs are reduced.

The most common types of seam

Open or plain seam
- the most common seam
- a flat seam that can be easily altered
- used on most types of textile items, such as household textiles and clothing
- raw edges need to be neatened, with, for example, a zigzag finish, to prevent fraying.

Double-stitched seam
- also known as the flat-fell seam
- stitched twice, therefore very strong
- all raw edges are enclosed
- double stitching forms a decorative feature
- used on jeans, overalls and pyjamas.

French seam
- stitched twice, therefore very strong
- all raw edges are enclosed
- used on fine, sheer fabrics, for example, on lingerie.

Overlaid seam
- stitching is visible and forms a decorative feature
- strong seam
- edges need to be neatened to stop fraying
- used on shirts or blouses, for example, to join a yoke piece.

Open or plain seam

What it looks like

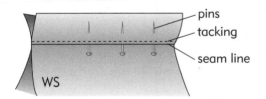

pins
tacking
seam line

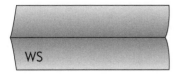

reverse machining to finish ends

Open or plain seam

How the seam is made

1 The fabrics are placed right sides (RS) together, and are then pinned and tacked.

2 The pins are removed and the seam is machine stitched 15 mm from edge of the fabric.

3 Loose threads are cut close to fabric. Tacking threads are removed.

4 Raw edges of the seam are neatened, for example by zigzagging or overlocking.

Double-stitched seam

What it looks like

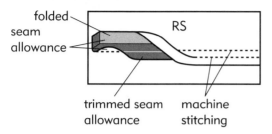

Double-stitched seam

How the seam is made

1 The fabrics are placed wrong sides (WS) together, and are then pinned and tacked.

2 The pins are removed and the seam is machine stitched, 15 mm from edge of the fabric.

3 The seam is pressed open and one side is cut to 5 mm.

4 The other side is folded inwards by 5 mm and ironed over the trimmed side.

5 The folded edge is pinned, tacked and machine stitched.

French seam

What it looks like

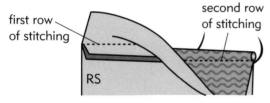

French seam

How the seam is made

1 The fabrics are placed wrong sides (WS) together, and then pinned and tacked.

2 The pins are removed and the seam is machined stitched 10 mm from the edge of the fabric.

3 The seam is pressed open and trimmed to 3–5 mm.

4 The fabric is folded so that the right sides (RS) are together, with the join exactly on the fold.

5 The seam is pinned, tacked and machine stitched on the original seam line 5 mm from edge.

Overlaid seam

What it looks like

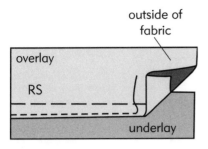

Overlaid seam

How the seam is made

1 A seam allowance of 15 mm is folded to the wrong side (WS) of one piece of fabric.
2 The folded edge is placed on the 15 mm stitching line of the second piece of fabric.
3 The seam is edge stitched close to the folded edge.
4 The seam is pressed and the raw edges trimmed to 10 mm.
5 The raw edges are neatened to prevent fraying.

Using Aesthetic and Creative Techniques

It is useful to have an understanding of the range of aesthetic and creative techniques used to **embellish** a fabric or product. You may need to apply this knowledge to an examination question by showing or explaining how a product could be improved using these techniques. They can be divided into two categories: colouring fabric and decorating with fabric, thread and other components.

Colouring fabric

Colour can be added to a fabric in the following of ways:

- While the fibres are in liquid form. This can only be done with man-made fibres and is known as spin dyeing.
- Before the fibres are spun into yarn, which is known as stock dyeing.
- Before the fabric is used, which is known as piece dyeing.
- At the end of the making stage, when the process is known as garment dyeing.

There are many different ways to colour and enhance or improve a fabric. There are four common techniques: **dyeing**, batik, fabric painting and spraying, and printing. There are also three main types of industrial dyeing processes: continuous, semi-continuous and batch dyeing.

Dyeing

Dyes can be divided into two types, both of which require a **mordant**:

- natural dyes made from natural sources like plants and animals
- synthetic dyes made cheaply from chemicals to produce a greater range of colours.

Tie-dye

Tie-dye is the simplest and most traditional method of colouring a fabric. It is a resist form of dyeing: the fabric is folded and tied with string or elastic bands to stop the dye reaching some parts of the fabric. After the fabric has been dyed, it is rinsed and dried. Tie-dye works best on a natural fabric, which should be washed first to remove any finishes.

Key word

Embellish means to decorate or improve the appearance of a fabric or product.

Key words

Dyeing is the immersion of fibres or fabrics into a liquid pigment to change their colour.

Mordant is a chemical used to fix the colour to the fabric.

No two patterns are the same. Different effects can be achieved by folding, pleating, rolling, re-folding between colours, adding knots, buttons and pebbles to the fabric to create complex patterns. Various techniques are commonly used.

Knotting – knots are tied in the fabric at random before dyeing.

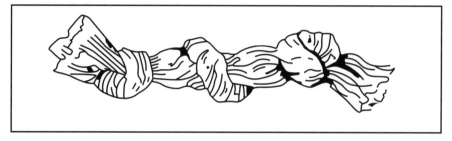

Folding and binding – the fabric is bound with string or elastic bands at intervals after it has been concertina-folded.

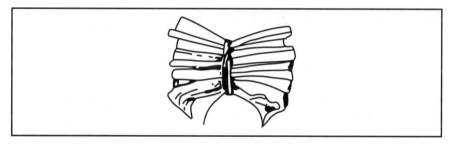

Twisting and binding – the centre of the fabric is pinched to a point and tied, and the remainder of the fabric is tied at intervals.

Marbling – the fabric is crumpled and tightly tied with string or elastic bands.

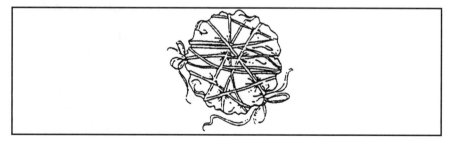

Batik

Batik originates in Indonesia, on the island of Java. It is a resist form of dyeing in which wax stops the dye reaching some parts of the fabric. The wax is applied to the fabric with a paint brush, stamp or tjanting tool to create a design. The fabric is then either immersed in a cold-water dye bath or dyes can be painted onto the surface where needed and left to dry. Finally, the wax is removed by ironing the fabric between two pieces of absorbent paper. Batik works best on a natural fabric, which should be washed first to remove any finishes. Popular effects include cracking and reverse batik.

Cracking or veining – all the fabric is covered with wax, allowed to dry and then cracked and crunched before dyeing. Lighter dyes should be used before darker ones for this method.

Reverse batik – all the fabric is covered with wax, allowed to dry and then the wax is scratched or scraped off the areas where the design is required before dyeing. Finer designs can be achieved using this method.

Fabric painting and spraying

Colour can be added to a fabric simply and directly using the following:

- **Fabric paints**
  - non-toxic
  - can be applied using a paint brush, airbrush or sponge for texture
  - fabric needs to be ironed when dry to fix the colour before washing.

- **Transfer crayons and marker pens**
  - non-toxic
  - clean and quick to use
  - fabric needs to be ironed on the reverse side to fix the colour before washing.

- **Spraying**
  - a speckled effect can be created on the surface of the fabric by using a spray diffuser or an airbrush
  - areas can be masked off using a stencil or colours can be blended together
  - the fabric needs to be ironed when dry to fix the colour before washing.

Printing

There is a range of different printing methods used to create designs on fabric. The most common types are screen, block, roller, transfer and flock printing.

Screen printing – is the most widely used method of printing on fabric. It is achieved in the following way:

1 a fine mesh of fabric, such as organdie or organza, is stretched over a frame and secured

2 the dye is moved across the screen using a squeegee, which forces the dye through the screen to the fabric beneath.

A screen can be used for:

- One-off prints – areas of the screen can be blocked off with a paper stencil.

- Long runs – a permanent screen is made using *either*
  a light-sensitive chemicals to block the areas where no dye is required, *or*
  b an insoluble polymer is used that can be etched away where the design is needed by a computer controlled laser beam.

> **Key word**
>
> **Screen printing** is the printing of a pattern on to fabric through a stencilled screen.

Block printing – is a technique which uses blocks made from a resistant material like wood to create a design. Dye is applied to the carved block and this is then pressed on to the fabric.

Roller printing – is the industrial development of block printing. The design is engraved on to the surface of copper rollers, so it is in relief. Therefore the design can only be the same width as the roller and a separate roller is needed for each colour in the design. This is an expensive process and is therefore only used if large amounts of fabric are to be printed.

Transfer printing – involves the printing of the reversed design on paper first. The design is then transferred to the fabric using heat, usually from a hot iron. In industry, the design is transferred to the fabric using heated rollers. The heat changes the dye on the paper to a gas, which attaches to the fabric as a colour and is fixed by the combination of heat and the pressure of the rollers. The two most common forms of transfer printing use:

- transfer printing inks or crayons
- a computer with special transfer paper in the printer.

Flock printing – is a technique where adhesive is printed onto the fabric. The fabric is then covered with cut fibre pieces which adhere to the adhesive to form a textured finish.

Industrial methods of dyeing

There are three main types of industrial dye processes: continuous, semi-continuous and batch dyeing.

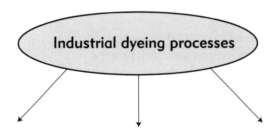

Industrial dyeing processes

Continuous dyeing
- also known as pad dyeing
- the whole of the fabric is placed in a pad bath with dye
- the fabric is squeezed to ensure dye is evenly spread.

Semi-continuous dyeing
- fabric is dyed and wound up on a batching roller to remove excess dye
- the dye is allowed to fix in the fabric on the roller.

Batch dyeing
- fabric is placed in a dye bath and allowed to absorb the dye.

There are three main types of batch dyeing: the jigger and winch systems and jet-dyeing.

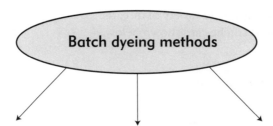

Jigger system
- the fabric is pulled backwards and forwards through the dye
- colour is evenly spread
- most successful with medium to heavy weight woven fabric, like twill.

Winch system
- the winch pulls the fabric through the dye in a circular movement
- most suitable for knitted and light weight woven fabrics, like silk.

Jet-dyeing
- the fabric is moved around in the dye using high pressure jets
- dyes are injected into the fabric in certain positions to create a design
- most useful for dyeing carpets.

Decorating with fabric, thread and components

There are five common techniques: appliqué (including molar work), embroidery (hand and machine), pleating and folding, quilting, and smocking.

Appliqué

This technique is often referred to as basic **appliqué** and involves the cutting out of shapes from one fabric and stitching them on to a background fabric. The shapes are usually backed with iron-on interfacing (Vilene) to strengthen them and prevent fraying. A close machine zigzag stitch is used to attach the shapes to the background fabric. Appliqué is used to:

- add texture and interest to a product

- strengthen and reinforce the fabric.

Types of appliqué:

- **Padded appliqué** – shapes can be padded by cutting the background fabric under the shape and pushing in filling. The gap is then hand stitched together.

- **Molar work** – also known as mola, molas, San Blas or reverse appliqué. This is where several layers of fabric are placed on top of each other and a design is outlined in stitching. Sections of the fabric are cut away close to the stitching through different numbers of layers revealing the fabrics beneath.

- **Appliqué Perse** – is where a printed shape or design, such as a flower, from one fabric is cut out and machine stitched on a background fabric.

41

Embroidery

Embroidery can be done either by hand or with a machine.

Hand embroidery – is a traditional craft using a wide variety of threads, fabrics and stitches. The most frequently used stitches are shown below.

Name of stitch	What it looks like
Straight stitch	
Blanket stitch	
Chain stitch	
French knot	
Couching	
Herringbone stitch	

Shisha work – is an Indian technique used for decorating fabrics by hand and involves stitching tiny mirrors on the fabric.

Free machine embroidery – uses a sewing machine to create a design on the fabric using the following method.

1 The presser foot is removed and the feed dog disengaged.

2 The fabric is stretched tightly on an embroidery hoop.

3 The fabric is then placed under the machine needle and the presser foot lever is lowered.

4 The fabric is moved around under the needle to get the required design.

5 Different stitches can be used to fill the areas, such as zigzag and straight stitch.

Computerised embroidery

Electronic sewing machines with scanners can be used to create logos and motifs on a garment using memory cards.

Computer-aided embroidery machines (e.g. POEM machines) have developed further because of better software packages and equipment. They allow images, photographs and drawings to be customised and digitised before being embroidered on a product. In industry, tubular (cylinder arm) machines or multi-head tubular system machines allow embroidery to be stitched on the made-up product.

Pleating and folding

These techniques can create interesting textural effects as well as give shape to a textile product. Pleats and folds can be pressed in place using an iron or can be stitched. There are three common types of pleats: knife, inverted and box pleat.

a)

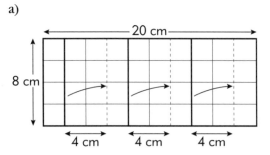

b)

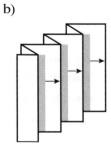

Knife pleat: a) pleat layout and b) method of folding

a)

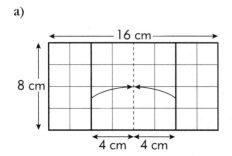

b)

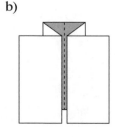

Inverted: a) pleat layout and b) method of folding

a)

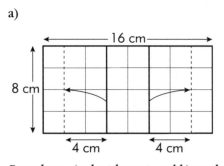

b)

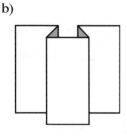

Box pleat: a) pleat layout and b) method of folding

It is important to know what each of these pleats looks like, what they are called, how they are worked and where they are used, for your written examination paper.

Quilting

This technique involves the stitching of the following three layers of fabric together.

1 decorative surface fabric

2 insulating fabric, such as wadding

3 cheaper bottom fabric, such as cotton sheeting.

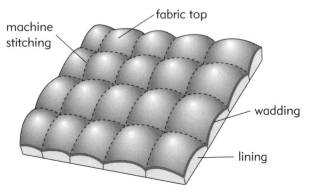

Quilting

The layers are placed together in the order above and are then pinned, tacked and machine stitched together. Quilting is used because it:

• gives a fabric better insulation and protective properties

• adds decoration to a fabric using a variety of stitching and patterns.

Smocking

This technique involves the pleating of fabric at regular intervals and hand stitching the top folds of the pleats to secure them and create a design.

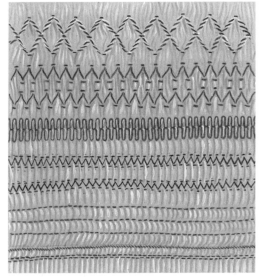

Smocking

Using Functional Finishes

Finishing edges

Edges of fabric need to be finished in some way for two specific reasons:

• to neaten the appearance of a product

• to prevent fraying and strengthen a product.

the use of seam finishes such as zigzag stitching

overlocking

the use of bias binding

Commonly used methods of finishing edges

facings and interfacing

hems

Overlocking

How it is done
- with an overlocking machine or overlocker, which stitches the seam, neatens the edge and cuts off the excess in one operation.

Advantages
- very versatile method which can be used on any raw edge
- suitable for finishing the edges of stretch fabrics
- a very neat and secure finish is achieved.

Bias binding

How it is done
- made from narrow strips of fabric cut on the cross of a woven fabric
- it is stitched on the right side (RS) of the product and then turned to the inside where it is stitched again by hand or machine.

Advantages
- a visible edge finish which can be decorative as well as functional
- it is slightly stretchy and therefore suitable for stitching around curved edges like armholes
- it will not wrinkle when stitched in position
- a very neat and strong edge finish.

Facings and interfacings

How it is done
- a facing is a piece of fabric cut to match the shape of the edge
- the raw edges of the facing are neatened, usually with an interlocker
- interfacing can be applied to strengthen and stiffen the facing so that it keeps its shape.

Advantages
- an invisible form of neatening an edge
- can be used to finish necklines and other openings.

Hems

The type of hem used depends on the fabric and style of the product. There are three common types.

Rolled hem – is mainly used on medium- to light-weight fabrics like linen and cotton. It is made in the following way:

1 a narrow hem is folded over twice

2 it is then secured by pressing or tacking the edge

3 the final fold may be machine stitched or hand stitched using a slip hemming stitch.

Single fold hem – is suitable for thicker fabrics like twill weaves. It is made as follows:

1 the raw edge is zigzag stitched or overlocked to neaten it

2 the hem is then folded once and secured by hand or machine stitching

3 any fullness may be gathered or pleated to make the hem flat.

Single fold hem using Bondaweb – is made in the following way:

1 the Bondaweb, a soft, fusible fleece, is placed between the folded hem and the main fabric

2 the fabric is then ironed so that the fleece melts and glues the hem securely in place.

Disposing of fullness

When using fabric for three-dimensional products such as garments, it often has to go around irregular or curved shapes, such as an armhole or a waistband. The resulting excess fabric or fullness needs to be reduced in size to ensure a quality finish and still allow for ease of movement.

cut the fabric to the required shape

make darts in the fabric

Ways to reduce fullness

put pleats or tucks in the fabric

gather the fabric

Darts

The main points to remember about **darts** are that they:

- usually start where a seam is to be made
- always taper to a point at the fullest part of the required shape
- are mainly used in waistlines and the bust lines of dresses and blouses
- can be single or double pointed.

Key word

A **dart** is a fold in the fabric which ends in a point at the fullest part of the shape.

A dart is made by:

1 matching the dots on the pattern piece, folding along the centre of the dart with the right side (RS) of the fabric facing

2 machine stitching using a straight stitch.

Making a dart

Tucks and pleats

These are folds in the fabric usually held in place by machine stitching, which can be decorative as well as functional. They are most often used in waistlines and for valances.

Gathers

The gathering of fabric can be achieved using gathering stitches or elastic.

Gathering – can be done by hand or machine. It involves the working of one or two rows of stitching. The threads are pulled carefully, easing the fabric along the thread to form even tucks of fabric. A gathering or ruffler attachment can be used on the sewing machine to speed up the process. Gathering are often used around cuffs, waistbands, sleeve heads and on yokes.

Elastic – can be threaded through a tube casing made in the fabric to gather a product. It allows a garment to be put on and taken off easily.

Key points

- Pinning, tacking and fastenings are temporary methods of joining fabrics.
- A seam is a permanent method of joining two pieces of fabric together.
- A seam allowance is the extra margin, usually 15 mm, required to prevent the seam being too close to the edge of the fabric.
- Aesthetic and creative techniques involve the use of fabric, thread, other components and colouring media.
- Colour can be introduced at any stage in the production of a textile item.
- A wide range of printing methods are used in industry.
- Pleating and smocking are decorative methods of shaping a product.
- Many textile products need to be shaped to dispose of fullness which can be achieved by using darts, tucks, pleats or gathers.

Questions

1 Choose one of the seams listed in this section. Explain, using diagrams and notes, how your chosen seam is worked.

2 Find an illustration of a textile product where the type of seam you have chosen would be used. List the reasons why the seam would be suitable for your chosen product.

3 The diagrams below show three different seams which could be used to join the side of a sports bag.

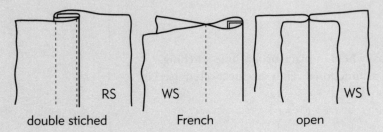

double stiched   French   open

Using diagrams and notes explain/show how each seam is worked (made).

4 Choose the most suitable seam to join the fabric at the position shown and justify your decision.

sports bag

Name of seam   . . . .

Reason: . . . .

. . . .

5 Suggest an alternative closing method to the one used in the sports bag above

a Closing method   . . . .

b Explain how to attach this to the sports bag   . . . .

. . . .

. . . .

ICT applications

This section will cover:

- What is ICT?
- CAD/CAM in industry
- Manufacturing using CAD/CAM
- Using computers to control machines
- Using ICT in textile technology activities.

What is ICT?

ICT (information communications technology) is the use of electronic devices such as a computer to communicate information. It is used extensively in industry to design and make products.

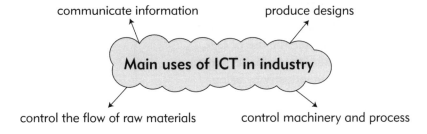

In the written examination, you will be expected to have a good understanding of the applications of ICT in designing and making textile products.

CAD/CAM in industry

CAD/CAM is one application of ICT that is especially relevant to the textile industry.

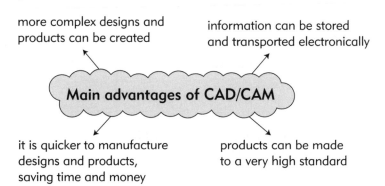

The main disadvantages of using CAD/CAM are:

- high initial costs to buy and set up specialist equipment
- some skilled workers may be necessary.

Key word

CAD stands for computer aided design.

CAM stands for computer aided manufacture.

Manufacturing using CAD/CAM

CAD/CAM is used to manufacture single items, such as garment prototypes and industrial mood boards, or batch products, such as T-shirts for a particular retail outlet. Designers and manufacturers in the textile industry now use computers and software packages to do hundreds of tasks that would have been done by hand in the past. These include:

- importing images from other equipment such as scanners and digital cameras or from the Internet
- cutting and pasting text, fabric, designs and images to create a variety of layouts, such as an attribute analysis on a mood board for a client
- editing and revising work until the designer and manufacturer are satisfied with the modifications
- automating repetitive tasks, such as repeat patterns for a fabric print
- creating accurate prototypes or toiles for textile products
- communicating design and manufacturing ideas electronically, using e-mail
- controlling the manufacture of items, using output devices such as a die cutter to stamp out pattern pieces or an industrial machine to embroider.

Using computers to control machines

Computer systems can control machines and equipment and simulate robotics used in a production line. For example, see the use of CNC machinery in commercial production on page 25. In the classroom it is easier to replicate the way a computer is used in industry by using:

- computerised embroidery and sewing machines
- computerised knitting machines
- microscopes for viewing and saving fabric construction details for further use
- scanners and digital cameras
- cutter and plotter machines for stencil work
- graphics tablets for creating and reproducing diagrams and drawings
- A3 printers for modelling and applying fabric designs to objects by transfer printing.

The use of CAD/CAM to manufacture single items and small batches is discussed on page 25.

Using ICT in textile technology

You should have an awareness of how to use ICT in various ways to design and manufacture textiles.

Desktop publishing

Desktop publishing (DTP) is most successful for combining written text with graphics, for example to produce a questionnaire to aid market research.

Producing charts and diagrams

Bar charts, pie charts and radar diagrams are a quick way of presenting data visually. They are useful to compare groups of data and, once the data has been entered, can be produced automatically by software, such as Microsoft Excel or other spreadsheet packages.

Producing graphics

It is possible to draw and modify anything on a computer. Paint and draw programs will produce original artwork, which can include lines, texture and colour. Texture mapping is also useful to experiment with different colour swatches on a design idea.

Graphics tablets can also be used to create designs. Objects can be moved on screen, which is particularly useful for fashion drawing and mood board presentation.

Manipulating text and graphics

Text and graphics in different font styles and size can be used to enhance the presentation and labelling of work.

Using ICT to aid design and technologies activities

You should be able to use ICT appropriately to handle, model or communicate design proposals. You should have an understanding of the following key areas:

- research from a database and using the Internet, for example take a look at www.british-shops.co.uk
- presentation of data using spread sheets, graphs, charts and graphics
- use of a spreadsheet for costing, modelling and fabric analysis
- use of a word processing package to create flow charts and production plans
- trialling of pattern ideas and layouts, for example using specialist CD-ROMs
- presentation of two-dimensional design pages and realistic representations.

Key points

- The main advantages of CAD/CAM are:
  - more complex designs can be created
  - information can be stored and transported electronically
  - it is quicker to manufacture designs and products
  - products can be made to a very high standard.
- The main disadvantages of CAD/CAM are:
  - high initial costs to buy and set up equipment
  - the need for a skilled workforce.
- You should be able to use CAD/CAM to:
  - desktop publish
  - produce text and graphics
  - present result in a graphical form
  - aid design and technology activities.

Questions

1 What do the initials CAD stand for?

2 What do the initials CAM stand for?

3 What do the initials DTP stand for?

Industrial applications

Commercial production methods

The three types of production are **job production**, **batch production** and mass or flow production.

Job production

This type of production method may also be referred to as one-off production, jobbie or jobbing.

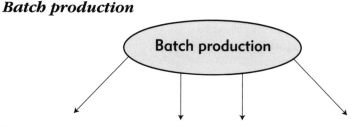

Job production

What it is
- a traditional method of production
- one unique item is made.

What it involves
- one operator or team makes the whole of the textile product
- highly skilled operators.

Advantages
- work is detailed and extensive
- versatile machinery is used to cover any textile process
- a high quality product made.

Problems
- high through-put time (it takes a long time to make)
- labour intensive
- very expensive.

Batch production

Batch production

What it is
- the production of a specific number of a product
- can be repeated as many times as needed.

What it involves
- workers can be organised into sections or cells to deal with a specific function, for example sewing a sleeve.

Advantages
- it is flexible and can easily be changed for new orders
- a variety of styles can be made
- more flexible working conditions
- training can be available for staff
- lower production costs.

Problems
- equipment needs to be re-started after a production run
- time is lost for changes
- storage of stock.

Mass or flow production

This type of production is also known as volume production and can be divided into two catagories: repetitive flow and continual flow production, both which are synchronised or straight-line systems.

Key word

Mass production is the production of a large number of identical items.

Repetitive flow production

What it is
- a large number of identical items are produced at a relatively low cost.

What it involves
- production is broken down into sub-assemblies of smaller components.

Advantages
- materials can be bought in bulk
- costs are lower
- semi-skilled and unskilled labour can be used
- a fully automated system.

Problems
- expensive to set up initially.

Continual flow production

What it is
- production of a textile item 24 hours a day.

What it involves
- uninterrupted production of an identical textile product.

Advantages
- reduced costs
- small workforce needed.

Problems
- expensive to shut down and re-start production.

Commercial manufacturing systems

It is important that you also have an understanding of the following commercial manufacturing systems:
- cell production
- in-line assembly
- 'just-in-time'
- 'off the peg' manufacture
- logistics.

Cell production

Also known as the section system, this type of production is where:
- teams or cells work separately on the different processes or components that combine to make a product
- all cells are situated close together
- product changes are easy to do.

Key word

Cell production is when teams work separately to make a product.

53

In-line assembly

In this system products that have many components are produced on a continuous assembly line. They are fully automated to ensure they are quick, efficient and produce quality products.

Key word

In-line assembly is a linear assembly line.

'Just-in-time'

This type of production requires regular deliveries of materials and components from suppliers, which arrive 'just-in-time' and are used immediately. Problems are caused if delay in the arrival of materials or components brings production to a halt. However, there are also advantages.

Key word

'Just-in-time' is when components and materials arrive as they are needed.

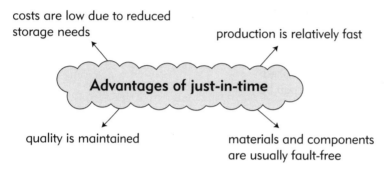

'Off-the-peg' manufacture

'Off-the-peg' garments are made to fit standard average sizes, not a particular individual. One standard size template is used for a production run and no fitting is necessary. This allows a batch of products to be made at one time and most of the production methods in this section will produce garments in this way.

Logistics

This is the transportation of materials and components into a factory and finished goods out again. The efficient production of a textile product can depend greatly on the availability of the required materials and components.

Key word

Logistics is the practice of moving materials and components to the correct place as and when they are needed.

Labelling, packaging, marketing and advertising

In considering the implication of these factors on a textile product, it is important to consider each one separately.

Labelling

The purpose of labelling is to help:

- provide information to the consumer e.g. fire hazards

- textile manufacturers in the European Union (EU) by keeping the names of fibres and the method of labelling consistent

- with stock control in retail outlets.

It is useful to remember that:

- the retailer has the responsibility for making sure goods offered to the public are labelled
- fibre content may be shown on a textile product by using:
  - a permanent label
  - a gummed label attached to the packaging
  - a ticket attached to the product.
- fibre content labelling is compulsory under the Textile Products (Indications of Fibre Content) Regulations 1986.

Smart labelling – it is important to be aware that advances in technology have led to more efficient systems in product labelling.

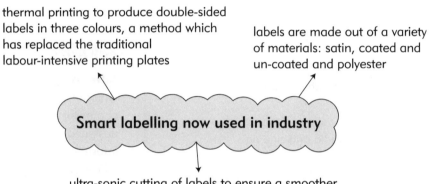

thermal printing to produce double-sided labels in three colours, a method which has replaced the traditional labour-intensive printing plates

labels are made out of a variety of materials: satin, coated and un-coated and polyester

Smart labelling now used in industry

ultra-sonic cutting of labels to ensure a smoother, neater edge, which reduces irritation for the user

Smart tagging – radio frequency identification (RFID) tagging has been developed to enhance the existing bar code identification systems.

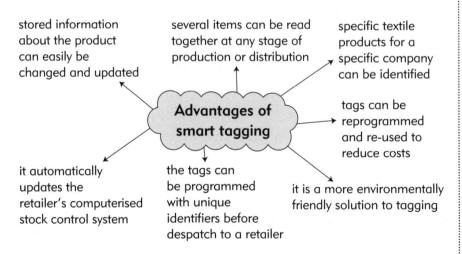

stored information about the product can easily be changed and updated

several items can be read together at any stage of production or distribution

specific textile products for a specific company can be identified

Advantages of smart tagging

tags can be reprogrammed and re-used to reduce costs

it automatically updates the retailer's computerised stock control system

the tags can be programmed with unique identifiers before despatch to a retailer

it is a more environmentally friendly solution to tagging

Packaging

Packaging is needed to:

- protect the product
- inform the consumer
- promote the product.

There are many examples of packaging in the shops and they use an extensive range of materials such as paper, cardboard and plastic. Many packages are designed to have a short life span and are often thrown away after purchase, which raises issues about the type and amount of material used and how well it can be recycled.

Marketing

This primarily involves finding out what people need and are prepared to buy, by:

- products: marketing viable products

- prices: setting realistic prices

- promotion: promoting the products

- place: selecting a suitable place to sell them.

These four words, starting with 'p', are often referred to as the 'marketing mix'.

Advertising

Large manufacturers employ advertising agencies to run their advertising campaigns. They use different media to attract different groups of consumers.

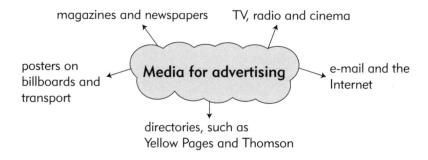

The Advertising Standards Agency (ASA) – regulates all British advertising in non-broadcast media. Their code of practice has three basic points which state that advertisements should:

- be legal, decent, honest and truthful

- show responsibility to the consumer and society

- follow business principles of fair competition.

Control as a necessary part of production and marketing

Control is a necessary part of production and marketing, and smart tagging is starting to address the issue. Appropriate controls must ensure that:

- a quality product, through quality guarantees, consumer rights and recognised standards, such as the BSI symbol or ISO 9000 as discussed on page 90.

- the consumer is satisfied with the product

- the product meets the criteria listed in the specification.

Key points

- The three types of commercial production methods are job, batch and mass or flow production.
- Mass or flow production can be divided into: repetitive flow and continual flow production.
- Commercial manufacturing systems include cell production, in-line assembly and 'just-in-time'.
- Packaging has three functions:
  - to sell the product
  - to protect the product
  - to communicate information to the consumer.
- Marketing – the marketing mix is:
  - right product
  - right price
  - in the right place
  - using the most suitable promotion.
- Fibre content labelling is compulsory by law in the EU.
- Tagging of textile products is used to help with effective stock control in retail outlets.

Activities

1. Produce a revision sheet explaining what you understand about each of the three commercial production methods. Present your results to a friend or small group in the class.

2. Select an example of packaging and show how it has been successfully used to fulfil the three main functions of:
   - selling the product
   - protecting the product
   - communicating information.

3. Choose one of the manufacturing systems that interests you. Discuss the advantages and disadvantages of a manufacturing company adopting this system.

Product evaluation

This section will cover:

- What is product evaluation?
- Quality assurance techniques
- Evaluating the proposed product
- Reviewing the use of materials and resources
- Testing.

What is product evaluation?

It is not just the product that needs to be evaluated, the process of designing and making it also needs to be considered. In the examination, you will need to evaluate your own designs and the work of others by looking at existing products. This section outlines the most important things to be considered when evaluating a product.

In industry, the evaluation process of designing and making a textile product is known as reviewing and refining. The aim of a review is to improve the quality and efficiency of a system and this often involves refining and adjusting the final product until all criteria are satisfied.

Quality assurance techniques

These are methods for checking that the required standard of manufacture has been met. It is important to review work at critical points and consider quality assurance techniques.

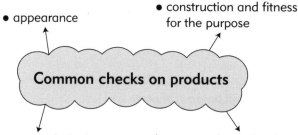

- appearance
- construction and fitness for the purpose

Common checks on products

- measurements and whether the size is correct
- tolerance and specification suitability of materials and components (whether the correct components have been used for the task)

There are many more quality assurance techniques used in industry, which involve the use of specialist equipment and each one helps to grade the quality of a textile product. A basic grading structure would be:

1 acceptable quality – the product matches the specification
2 rework – the product does not meet the specification but can be reworked, for example a hem can be machined again
3 reject – the product cannot be modified in order to meet the specification and so must be discarded, for example when the fabric is torn.

Evaluating the proposed product

It is important that you are able to evaluate a product against the following criteria:

- the specification

- its fitness for the purpose

- the design need

- the needs of the intended user(s)

- the quality and effective use of materials and resources

- the moral, cultural and environmental issues relevant to the user(s).

Reviewing the use of materials and resources

You should be able to consider whether materials and resources have been used appropriately. Key considerations are whether:

- the material used is the most appropriate one

- the pre-manufactured components used are the most suitable

- the supply of materials and components, and the method of manufacture minimise waste.

Testing

You should be able to carry out testing and recommend or make necessary changes as a result. This might include changes or improvements to:

- the product
- the pattern, template or manufacturing control system, for example the pattern lay to improve production of a batch of T-shirts.

In industry, system evaluation is usually carried out in the following way:

1 all stages in the manufacturing process are listed

2 problem areas are highlighted

3 possible solutions are assessed

4 future improvements are suggested

5 alternative ways of making the product are listed, including the following issues:
    - use of a different system
    - use of different materials to reduce costs
    - improvement of quality
    - improvement of health and safety
    - environmental issues
    - accessibility to a range of users
    - implications on society, such as use of local materials.

When evaluating the performance of a manufacturing control system, ensure that it is appropriate to the actual product.

Key points

- Evaluation can be defined as a process to ensure that products match the specification criteria set.
- Quality assurance techniques should take place throughout manufacture.
- Reviewing is the evaluation of the designing and making process.
- Refining is making adjustments or modifications to a product based on evaluation evidence.
- Different products require different methods of testing. You should be able to devise strategies to improve the manufacturing system and the materials used.
- Always consider moral, social, cultural and environmental issues in evaluating your product.

Questions

1 List the critical points to consider when evaluating the proposed product.

2 Explain the process used in industry to grade the quality of a textile product.

3 State how a system evaluation is carried out in industry.

4 Explain what you understand by the terms 'reviewing' and 'refining'.

5 Discuss why it is important to evaluate a product against its intended purpose.

Knowledge and Understanding

Materials and pre-manufactured standard components

Fibres and Fabrics

This section will cover:

- Origin of natural and manufactured fibres
- Structure of natural and manufactured fibres
- Performance characteristics and the relationship between origin and structure of the fibre including:
  - how materials respond under different conditions depending on fibre content and structure
  - how textiles behave when they are worked with
- Conversion of fibres into fabrics, specifically by spinning, weaving, knitting and bonding
- How methods of construction affect the way fabrics behave
- Processes applied to fibres and fabrics during manufacture and how they affect the way fabrics behave
- How fibres and yarns can be mixed and blended to enhance physical and aesthetic properties.

Origin of natural and manufactured fibres

Natural

Plant
Cotton:
- is a cellulosic fibre
- fibres from the boll (seed pod) of the cotton plant.

Linen:
- is a cellulosic fibre
- fibres from the stem of the flax plant.

Animal
Wool:
- is a protein fibre
- fibres are animal hairs usually from sheep, but also camels, goats, llamas or rabbits.

Silk:
- is a protein fibre
- fibres from the silk worm.

 **Man-made (manufactured)**

Synthetic
- fibres are made entirely from chemicals
- chemicals used are derived from oil or coal.

Examples of synthetic fibres:
- polyamide (nylon)
- polyester
- acrylic
- elastane
- microfibres, moulded to be very fine.

Regenerated
- are cellulosic fibres
- are natural fibres modified by chemicals during manufacture.

Examples of regenerated fibres:
- viscose
- triacetate
- modal
- cupro
- acetate.

Cotton

Cotton plants need a tropical climate and wet soil for good growth. It is therefore grown mainly in China, USA, India and Pakistan.

The seed pod or boll develops after flowering and the cotton fibres grow around the seeds inside the boll. Then the outer casing cracks to reveal the cotton fibres. The bolls are processed in the following way to make yarn.

1 The ripe bolls are harvested by hand or machine.

2 Ginning – discards the seeds and other unwanted parts of the plant, and the fibres are sorted into short lengths (known as linters) and long lengths (known as lint). The fibres are then compressed into bales.

3 The fibres are then teased and loosened with rollers and beaters to remove impurities.

4 Jets of air move the fibres, fluffing and forming them into sheets known as laps.

5 The laps are passed into a scutcher which has a revolving beater to remove any further impurities.

6 Carding – pulls and brushes the fibres so they lie in the same direction.

7 Combing – stretches the fibres into a thin, loose rope called a sliver. These are twisted together, pulled and drawn out to form stronger slivers. The fibres are then combed.

8 Roving – mixes, stretches and twists approximately six slivers together. The slivers are then placed in machines that make the fibres even thinner ready to be spun into yarn.

Linen

Linen (or flax) plants grow well in cool, damp climates and the major producers are China, Russia, France and the Ukraine. They are processed in the following way.

1 The plants are harvested in July or August either by hand or machine. The roots are often taken as well to ensure a long stem.

2 Roughing out or rippling – removes the outer leaves, flowers and seeds.

3 Retting – the plant stems are soaked in warm water for five to eight days, rotting the outer stem. The fibres are removed and dried.

4 Scotching – machines with fluted rollers separate the fibres from the woody parts of the stem.

5 Hackling – fibres are combed by machine to straighten them. The longer fibres known as flax lines, are used to make twine. The other fibres are formed into slivers and processed into yarn in the same way as cotton fibres.

6 Bleaching – yarn from linen fibres is known as 'grey yarn' until it is bleached or boiled white and able to take dye.

Wool

Wool fibres are the hair of animals, usually sheep. Although sheep are found in almost every country in the world, the major wool producers are New Zealand, former USSR and China. The best soft, fine wool is from the merino sheep, which is a Spanish breed. Wool is produced in the following way.

1 Shearing – is done with electric shears.

2 Grading – the wool is graded according to fineness, crimp length, impurities and colour into four categories, from 1 for the best, to 4 for the worst.

3 Scouring – the fleece from the sheep is washed several times to remove soil, grease, twigs and sweat.

4 Spinning – either the woollen system, in which shorter fibres make hairy yarn, or the worsted system, in which longer fibres are processed to make a better, smoother yarn, can be used.

Woollen system

1 Fibres are mixed together and any impurities are removed.

2 Fibres are treated with oil to strengthen them for the spinning process.

3 Carding – fibres are passed through rollers with fine wires to comb the fibres into a web.

4 The web is divided into slivers, which are doubled and made into rovings ready for spinning.

5 Spinning – rovings are twisted together, pulled and twisted again to make the required thickness of yarn.

6 Yarns are then knitted or woven into fabric.

Worsted system

1 Longer wool fibres are mixed and treated with oil.

2 Fibres are carded – passed through a machine to comb them parallel to each other.

3 Gilling – fibres are passed through a gilling machine where they are pulled and thinned ready to be wound into balls.

4 Combing – fires are re-combed to improve the alignment and keep fibres parallel to each other.

5 Shorter fibres are removed to form slivers, which are made into rovings by twisting and pulling.

6 The final spinning process pulls and twists the fibres to the required thickness and strength.

7 The fibres are wound on to cones ready to be woven or knitted into fabric.

Silk

Silk fibres come from the cocoons of silkworms, the larvae of the *Bombyx mori* moth. Silkworms feed on the leaves of the mulberry tree, so silk can only be produced where the tree grows. The major silk producers are China, India, Japan and the former USSR. Silk is produced in the following way.

1 Spinning the cocoon – the silkworm feeds for approximately 30 days on mulberry leaves and grows to 8cm long. At this stage it starts to spin a cocoon. Glands in the silkworm produce a sticky protein called fibron which dries when it comes into contact with the air to form a silk fibre. Sericin, produced from two more glands, sticks the fibres together. The cocoon takes three days to complete.

Key word

Cultivated silk is made from the fibres of the cocoon of the mulberry silkworm.

2   If left to nature, the moth would emerge after 14 days, producing a substance to soften the cocoon and breaking the silk fibres into small lengths. However, for silk production, the pupa is killed with steam or hot air before the moth can emerge so that the fibres are kept undamaged.

3   The cocoons are then placed in hot water to loosen the gum.

4   The surface of the cocoon is gently brushed to find the end of the thread.

5   Threads of silk are wound on to a reel and are known as raw or greige silk. A reel is about 1000 metres of continuous filament and is ready to be made into yarn.

Nett silk

This is yarn made of the longer fibres and is used to make high grade, expensive silk fabrics. There are two types of nett silk:

- Organzine yarn consists of two or three lengths of raw silk twisted loosely together. It has a good lustre but little strength.

- Tram yarn consists of lengths of raw silk which are doubled and twisted to make them stronger. It is duller and stronger then organzine.

Spun silk

Waste silk fibres, shorter than the fibres used to make nett silk, are made into spun silk yarns or schappe silk. They are lower in quality and cheaper to produce and buy. Spun silk yarns are produced in the following way.

1   The fibres are washed and placed in a combing machine.

2   The fibres are cut to a uniform length of 15 cm and shorter fibres are removed.

3   The longer fibres are placed in a machine that makes them into a lap of 90 cm wide.

4   The lap is pulled to form slivers that are then drafted into rovings ready for spinning.

Noil silk

Noil silk (also known as bourrette silk) is made from silk fibres that are too short to be made into spun silk. They are coarse yarns that have no lustre and are used mainly for industrial purposes.

Wild silk

Tussah is one of the main wild silks to be processed. The cocoons, gathered from trees and bushes in the wild, are often broken because the moths have already emerged. The fibres differ from cultivated silk in that they are:-

- coarser and less even along the length
- heavier, with a hard, less regular feel
- less shiny
- more red/brown in colour.

Man-made fibres

The production of man-made fibres is similar to the way silkworms make silk.

1   A sticky, thick liquid is formed by mixing substances together.

2   This is forced through a device called a spinneret which produces strands of fibres, like water coming from a showerhead.

3   The fibres are solidified by using warm air, cold air or a special liquid.

4   They are then wound onto a bobbin ready for transportation.

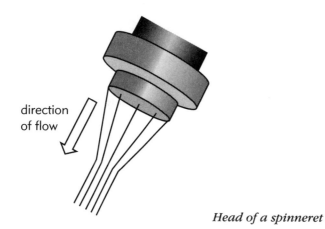

direction of flow

Head of a spinneret

Man-made fibres can be divided into two groups.

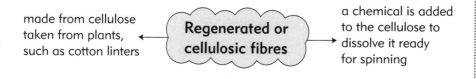

made from cellulose taken from plants, such as cotton linters

Regenerated or cellulosic fibres

a chemical is added to the cellulose to dissolve it ready for spinning

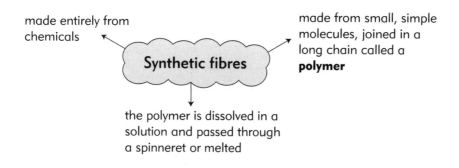

made entirely from chemicals

Synthetic fibres

made from small, simple molecules, joined in a long chain called a **polymer**

the polymer is dissolved in a solution and passed through a spinneret or melted

Key word

A **polymer** is a long chain of simple monomer units joined together.

Structure of natural and manufactured fibres

It is important to know about the structure of different fibres so that you can use a diagram to help you explain the performance characteristics of a fibre or fabric in your examination. The structure of the fibres is shown in the table below.

Performance characteristics

Performance characteristics	Structure of the fibres	Recognised symbol
Cotton fibres: • are fine, flexible and lie close together making cotton cool to wear • have low elasticity and therefore crease easily • absorb 65% of their own weight of water, making them strong and absorbent • wash well.	*Cotton fibres are shaped like a kidney bean or a figure of eight*	
Linen fibres: • are poor insulators because the smooth surface of the fibre prevents air being trapped • are cool to wear • are very absorbent, strong when wet and hardwearing • are less supple and firmer to handle than cotton • wash well and dry quickly.	*Linen fibres are irregular in shape and have ridges like bamboo along the length of the fibre*	
Wool fibres: • are resistant to creasing, comfortable to wear and have good elasticity because they are made from protein • insulate well because of the surface scales, crimp and length of the fibres, which trap and hold air. • are very absorbent, but slightly water repellent • can be easily moulded when warm and wet to form shaped products, such as hats, which means that care must be taken during washing.	*Wool fibres are round or oval with scales along the length; scales help with insulation, but cause problems when fibres are washed; the fibres have a natural crimp*	PURE NEW WOOL
Silk fibres: • have the unusual characteristic of being both cool and warm to wear because a small amount of air is trapped in the fabric, acting as an insulator while feeling cool next to the skin • are absorbent and dye well • are long and smooth which gives a very lustrous and soft finish • have good resistance and do not crease easily • are very strong.	*Silk fibres can be up to 3000 metres long; they are very smooth and have a rounded, triangular shape*	

Performance characteristics	Structure of the fibres
Viscose fibres: • are weaker when wet than when dry • crease easily • are smooth yarns that do not trap air easily, which makes them cool to wear • are very absorbent and comfortable to wear • take colour and dyes well.	*Viscose fibres look very similar to acetate fibres and vary slightly depending on the type of spinning used to make them*
Acetate fibres: • are naturally white and can be coloured easily • do not shrink or stretch and are not harmed by chemicals used in dry cleaning • are reasonably absorbent and crease resistant • triacetate fibres are thermoplastic and can be permanently creased or pleated, so they are often mixed with other fibres.	*Acetate fibres have ridges along their length, which differ depending on the type of spinning used to make them*
Polyamide (nylon) fibres: • trap little air and are therefore poor insulators • the chemical structure makes them resistant to mould and fungi, and they do not decompose • are thermoplastic so they can be permanently pleated or creased by applying heat • can be damaged by excessive heat, so care needs to be taken during ironing • are strong fibres that crease easily, are not absorbent and build up electrostatic charges.	*Polyamide fibres are usually smooth but the appearance varies depending on the spinneret*
Polyester fibres: • trap little air and are therefore poor insulators • absorb little water but transport it in the spaces between the fibres making the fabric more comfortable to wear next to the skin • are resistant to mould and fungi, and do not decompose • are thermoplastic so fabrics can be permanently pleated or creased and yarns textured.	*Polyester fibres are usually smooth but the appearance varies depending on the spinneret*
Acrylic fibres: • are thermoplastic but they can be damaged by heat and will shrink if washed at high temperatures or tumble dried • have low absorbency, dry quickly and are not damaged by sunlight • have low density making them lightweight and are easy to dye • recognised trade names: Acrylan, Courtelle, Draylon and Orlon.	a b *Acrylic fibres as seen under a microscope: a) cross-section and b) longitudinal*

Performance characteristics

Modacrylic fibres:

- are modified acrylic fibres that have similar characteristics to acrylic fibres

- are also flame-resistant making them useful for protective clothing and furnishing

- are also porous adding to their absorbency and making them more comfortable to wear.

Microfibres:

- are very fine fibres

- are often made from polyamide or polyester fibres

- are lightweight, strong, crease resistant, soft and drape well.

Conversion of fibres into fabrics

Spinning

Spinning twists a number of fibres, which brings them in contact with each other and creates a friction that holds them together. The number of times the yarn is twisted in a metre is known as the twist level. Then the yarn can be woven, knitted or bonded to make a fabric.

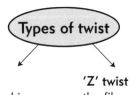

Types of twist

'S' twist
the fibres are twisted in an anti-clockwise direction

'Z' twist
the fibres are twisted in a clockwise direction

Weaving

The **weaving** of threads to produce fabric is done on a piece of equipment called a loom. A woven fabric is made with two sets of yarn:

Warp yarns – are strong threads and run along the length of the fabric (known as the straight grain).

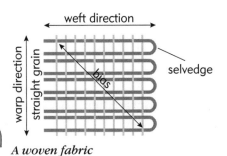

A woven fabric

Weft yarns – are interwoven at right angles to the warp threads, carried across by shuttle or a jet of air or water. left to right.

A **selvedge** is formed on each side edge of the fabric as the weft threads turn to go back the other way. It is strong, firm and does not fray.

Knitting

There are two types of knitting:

Weft knitting – produces a fabric made from one long length of yarn. The loops made in the yarn are interlocked with the loops above and below to form a fabric, and can be made by hand or machine.

Warp knitting – is done by machine and produces a fabric in which the loops made in the yarn are linked together from side to side.

Bonding

Bonded fabrics are classified as 'non-woven' fabrics. A bonded web is produced in the following way.

1 The fibres are positioned in one of four ways:

- they are blown by air so they fall in a random manner, known as random laid, or

- they are combed to lie straight, side by side, known as parallel laid, or

- they are laid at right angles to each other, known as cross laid, or

- they are pumped straight on to a conveyor belt, known as the spun bonded process.

2 The fibres in the web are then bonded, by using moisture, heat or pressure.

How methods of construction affect the way fabrics behave

Woven fabrics

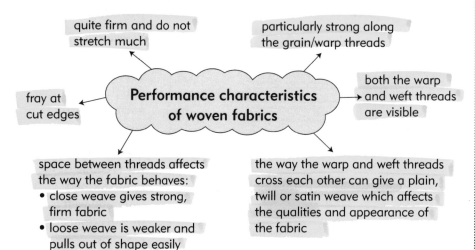

quite firm and do not stretch much

particularly strong along the grain/warp threads

Performance characteristics of woven fabrics

fray at cut edges

both the warp and weft threads are visible

space between threads affects the way the fabric behaves:
- close weave gives strong, firm fabric
- loose weave is weaker and pulls out of shape easily

the way the warp and weft threads cross each other can give a plain, twill or satin weave which affects the qualities and appearance of the fabric

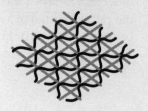

Characteristics	What it looks like
Plain weave – e.g. cotton fabric One weft thread over one warp thread • looks the same on both sides • creases and does not drape well • fairly hard wearing • has a plain, even surface.	
Twill weave – e.g. denim One weft thread over two or more warp threads • very hard-wearing fabric • definite right and wrong side • uneven surface • few wrinkles and good crease resistance • firm fabric likely to fray.	
Satin weave One weft thread over 4–8 warp threads • very smooth fabric • frays easily • not very hard-wearing • definite right and wrong side • will wrinkle and is quite stiff.	

> **Key word**
>
> **Performance characteristic** is the way a fabric or material functions to meet certain requirements.

Pile fabrics

Velvet, corduroy and terry towelling are all examples of pile fabrics. They have threads or loops on the surface.

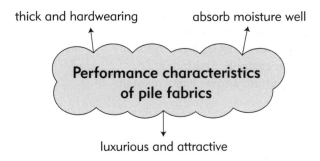

Knitted fabrics

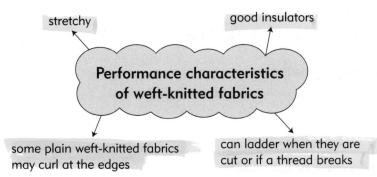

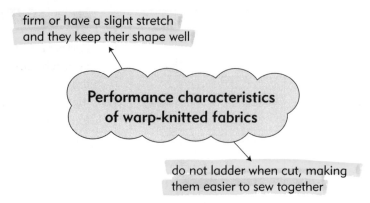

firm or have a slight stretch and they keep their shape well

Performance characteristics of warp-knitted fabrics

do not ladder when cut, making them easier to sew together

Bonded fabrics

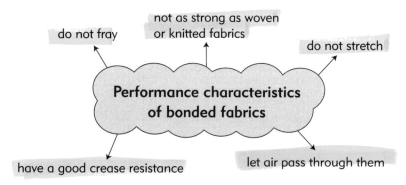

do not fray

not as strong as woven or knitted fabrics

do not stretch

Performance characteristics of bonded fabrics

have a good crease resistance

let air pass through them

Processes applied to fibres and fabrics and how they affect the way a fabric behaves

Physical or chemical processes can be applied to give a particular finish to fibres, yarns, fabrics or completed garments. Such finishes will improve the appearance, the feel or the wear of the finished fabric or garment. Some fabrics are given a combination of finishes. For example, children's nightwear may have a brushed fluffy pile for warmth and be flame-resistant for safety.

Physical finishes

Applied by a mechanical action which changes the fabric surface.

Brushing

- this process raises the surface of the fabric
- wire-covered rollers pull up the fibre ends to form a pile, giving a soft, fluffy surface
- air is trapped in the fibres giving good insulation.

Disadvantages:

- fabric is more flammable
- fabric can be weakened by the action of the rollers.

Used for: cotton bedding and garments such as nightwear.

Calendering

- this process smooths the surface of the fabric
- heated rollers compact the surface of the fabric, improving its lustre (shine)
- embosses patterns if engraved rollers are used
- a watermark effect can also be created.

Disadvantages:

- fabric requires dry cleaning; washing causes the fibres to swell and spoil the finish
- not a permanent finish, although it is durable.

Used for: furnishing fabric such as chintz.

Chemical finishes

Different chemical finishes can be applied to yarns and fabrics to give them particular characteristics.

Mercerising – sodium hydroxide is added to the fibres while they are held under tension. The process has a permanent effect. It makes the cotton fibres straighter and more rounded, making them softer, stronger, more absorbent and more lustrous. It is used for sewing threads, dress and shirt fabrics, and furnishing fabrics.

Flame proofing – chemicals, such as proban, are applied to the yarn or fabric to slow down or prevent burning. Fabrics become stiffer and need to be washed carefully. It can be used on any fabric and is especially useful on furnishing fabrics in public places.

Stain resistance – silicones can be applied so that fabric resists water-based stains or synthetic resins applied for resistance to oil-based stains. This also makes a fabric waterproof. Scotchguard is one example. The treatment is used to finish fabrics, floor coverings, shoes and clothing.

Easy care – chemicals can be applied to a fabric to make it easier to wash and iron, protect it against shrinkage and made it crease resistant. It is used on items made of cotton and viscose fibres.

Antistatic – Chemicals are applied to synthetic fibres to stop them clinging and attracting dust and dirt. The treatment is used on floor coverings, underwear and lingerie.

Anti-felting – wool fibres can felt or matt together if not washed correctly. An oxidative treatment can be used to soften the tips of the wool scales or a synthetic polymer film can be coated on to the fibre to stop felting and **pilling**.

Moth proofing – chemicals are applied to the fabric making the fibres inedible to moths and so repelling them. The treatment is used particularly on woollen fabrics.

Waterproofing – chemicals such as silicones are sprayed on the fabric or impregnated into it. Different levels of protection can be achieved and the treatment is invisible and renewable. It is used on outdoor clothing and fabric for items such as tents and umbrellas.

Key word

Pilling is the appearance of small balls of fibre on the surface of the fabric.

How fibres and yarns can be mixed and blended to enhance physical and aesthetic properties

First, it is important to know what is meant by the words 'mixture' and 'blend'.

Blend – different fibres are mixed together as the yarn is spun.

Mixture – one type of fibre is used for the warp thread and another for the weft. The mixing occurs during the weaving process.

Fabrics used for fashion and furnishings are often made from more than one type of fibre. This combines the desirable performance characteristics of the chosen fibres and can reduce the cost of production.

Advantages of school shirt made from a blend of cotton (C) and polyester (P):

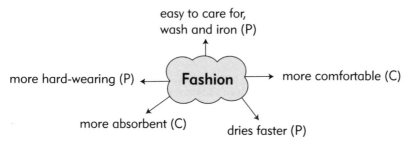

Advantages of curtains made from a synthetic and a natural fibre:

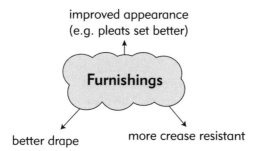

Enhancing the aesthetic properties of a fabric

Mixing different fibres at the weaving stage can:

- add texture to a fabric by using a textured yarn with a smooth yarn
- add colour variation by using coloured yarns to create stripes or checks
- give ribbed effects by weaving different thicknesses of yarns together
- enhance lustre or sparkle.

Enhancing the physical properties of a fabric

Mixing or blending fibres together can:

- make a fabric warmer or more comfortable to wear, usually by adding a natural fibre
- add strength and make a product more durable
- make a fabric more absorbent to sweat and moisture
- make it easier to care for, wash and iron
- improve the feel or touch of the fabric.

74

Key points

- Natural fibres come from plants and animals.
- There are four main types of natural fibre: cotton, silk, linen and wool.
- Man-made fibres do not occur naturally.
- Each fibre has different performance characteristics or properties which suit different textile products.
- The way the fibre is made into a yarn and the yarn made into fabric affects the performance characteristics of the finished fabric.
- Yarns can be woven, knitted or bonded to make a fabric.
- Yarns are fibres twisted together through a process known as spinning.
- Fibres and fabrics can be finished by physical or chemical methods.
- Finishes improve the appearance, the feel and/or the wear of the fabric.
- Fabrics can be made from more than one type of fibre.
- Fabrics made from a mixture or blend of fibres have improved physical and/or aesthetic performance characteristics.

Questions

1 Summarise the performance characteristics of a) silk fibres, b) acrylic fibres and c) acetate fibres.
2 List the main differences between a woven and a knitted fabric.
3 What is the main advantage of a bonded fabric?
4 Explain the difference between weft and warp knitted fabrics.
5 Describe the differences between physical and chemical finishes.

Pre-manufactured standard components

This section will cover:

- What pre-manufactured components are
- Components that perform a similar function
- Aesthetic and functional purposes of components
- How pre-manufactured components are used in industry.

What pre-manufactured components are

These components can be broken down into five main groups:

- thread
- fastenings
- linings and interfacings
- decorative components
- functional components.

Thread

Thread is used to join pieces of fabric together and also for decoration, such as top stitching. The threads used for sewing must match the fabric in both fibre and weight to produce a good quality product.

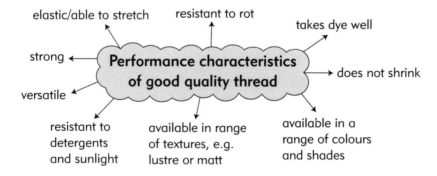

Most modern threads are made from one or a combination of the following.

- **Polyester** – has all the performance characteristics on the mindmap above.
- **Cotton** – is strong and versatile, but expensive.
- **Viscose** – is inexpensive, takes dyes extremely well and is used mainly for embroidery.
- **Linen**– is strong, versatile and dyes well to give exact colour, but is expensive and is used in one-off production.
- **Silk** – as linen.

Key word

Pre-manufactured components are items that are used on products in addition to fabric.

Fastenings

Most examination questions on fastenings are based on the reasons why a particular type is chosen for a product. You also need to know about fastenings for any design-and-make questions.

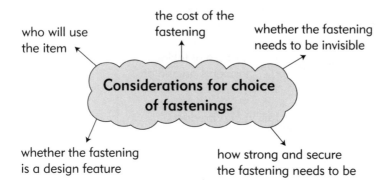

The main fastenings you need to know about are:

Zips – are used to fasten a textile product, allowing it to be opened and closed easily. They can be decorative or functional, are available in a variety of colours and lengths, can be open-ended for jackets or closed for skirts and trousers, and do not undo by accident easily.

Velcro – is made of two layers of nylon, one covered with tiny hooks which grip the tiny loops on the other piece when the two are pressed together. It is a secure, non-movable fastening which is easy and quick to use. It can be washed and dry cleaned, sterilised at high temperatures which is useful for hospital use, and its strength increases under pressure. It is a versatile fastening and is very useful for people with limited hand movement and strength, as well as being popular for the production of children's clothing and shoes.

Press fasteners and ginger snaps – are strong, secure, easy to fasten and unfasten, available in a range of sizes, and can be made from plastic or metal. Press fasteners (also known as press studs) are attached to a product using thread. Ginger snaps are attached using a special locking tool. These types of fasteners are often used on quilt covers or as a secondary form of fastening, for example on a skirt waistband with a zip.

Hooks and eyes – are a discrete form of fastening, which are strong, secure and are available in a variety of sizes and colours. They are often used at the top of zips to stop the garment coming off if the zip comes undone.

Buttons and buttonholes – provide a strong, secure, localised form of fastening and are the most popular of all fastenings. They can be flat or have a shank, are made with two or four holes and are attached to a product using thread. They can be decorative as well as functional and are available in a range of colours, sizes and shapes.

Linings and interfacings

These are used to provide support and insulation, and to improve the appearance of a textile product.

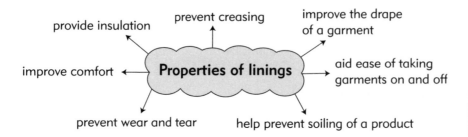

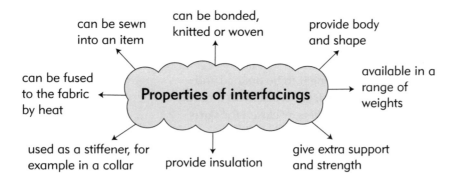

Components that perform a similar function

Buttons, Velcro and zips are all secure and strong forms of fastening, which can be decorative as well as functional, tight and, particularly in the case of Velcro and zips, waterproof.

Aesthetic and functional purposes of components

The main decorative components are:

- **Sequins and beads** – are used for surface decoration to add colour, texture and sparkle.

- **Braid, fringing, feathers, fur, lace and piping** – are used to add interest, texture, colour and often cover raw edges.

- **Embroidered or Appliqué motifs and badges** – can be used to enhance the appearance of an item and can be added or made either by hand or machine.

- **Buttons and zips** – can also be decorative, as well as functional, and used to add interest to an item.

Key words

Aesthetic (or decorative) components are used to decorate textile products.

Functional (or structural) components are used to give shape to textile products.

78

The main functional components are:

- **Boning** – is a strip of flexible polyester tape which is rigid when stitched into a textile item. Boning gives shape and structure to clothing, for example in the bodice of an evening gown.

- **Shoulder pads** – provide padding to redefine the shape of the shoulder line. They can be stitched between the lining and the outer fabric of a garment or attached inside the garment. They are used mainly in jackets, suits or coats.

- **Elastic** – this is used to reduce fullness in an item. It can be sewn directly on to the fabric, for example in the waistline of boxer shorts or inserted into a casing, for example on a skirt waistband.

How pre-manufactured components are used in industry

Pre-manufactured components are essential to commercial manufacturing systems such as 'just-in-time' production which need regular deliveries from suppliers. The components arrive just in time for the product to be made and are used straightaway. They are usually of the best quality because they have not been repeatedly moved in storage and transit.

Sewing threads are used in most fabric products. Silk or linen threads are more likely to be used in haute couture or one-off production because their performance characteristics will match the item being produced.

Components such as ready-made facings and cuffing can be produced quickly and efficiently by suppliers, ready for attaching to garments made at different manufacturing companies.

Key points

- Pre-manufactured components can be broken down into five main groups: threads, fastenings, linings and interfacings, decorative and functional components.

- Textile components which perform a similar function are Velcro and zips.

- Textile components can be decorative and/or functional.

- You should be able to describe the types of components frequently used on textile items and know how they function.

Activities

1 The illustration below shows the pattern pieces required to make a sports bag.

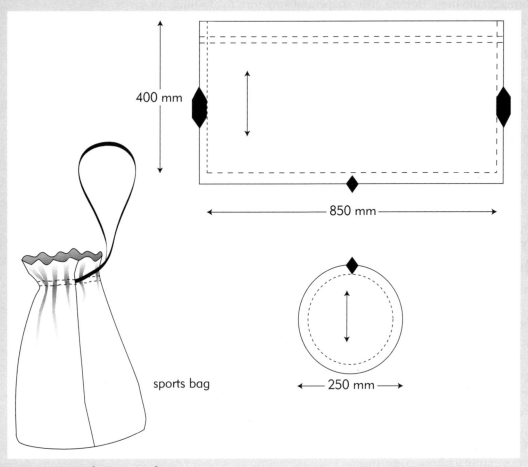

400 mm

850 mm

sports bag

250 mm

The pattern pieces for a sports bag

a Name two textile components that are required to make the bag.

b Suggest a suitable closing method, other than the drawstring handle, for fastening the sports bag. Explain how to attach this to the bag.

c Explain how the bag could be made more rigid.

2 You can use mnemonics to remember difficult things by turning the first letter of each word into something that you can remember, for example:

E G B D F = Every good boy deserves football.

Key words to remember	Have a try yourself
Thread	T
Fastenings	F
Linings and interfacings	L
Decorative	D
Functional	F

Smart and modern materials

This section will cover:

- Smart materials and their properties
- Further development of smart and modern materials.

Smart materials and their properties

Technological research involving scientists and textile designers working together has resulted in the development and production of a range of new fibres and fabrics, which have become known as smart and modern textiles. Chemicals, **encapsulation** and electronics are used to create these textiles, which can be used in a wide variety of specialised applications.

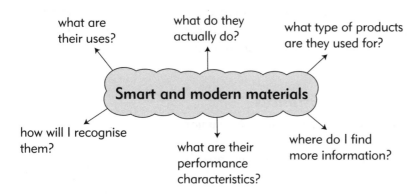

'Sense and react' materials

Materials that **sense and react** can be divided into three groups.

Passive smart – a material that senses the environmental conditions.

Active smart – a material that can sense and react to environmental conditions.

Very smart – a material that senses, reacts and adapts to environmental conditions.

These materials can be used in a wide range of very different products.

Medical textiles – pillows and mattresses that respond and mould to the shape of the sleeper.

Sportswear – ski suits that react to body temperature and can increase their insulating properties to make the body warmer.

Military uniforms – clothing that changes colour according to the environment to aid camouflage.

Sun suits – clothing that provides protection against the ultraviolet rays of the sun.

81

Materials that change colour

Different dyes and inks can be applied to materials so that they can change colour in response to heat, light or moisture.

Photo-chromic dyes – react to heat by changing colour. They work well on cotton or fabrics with a high percentage of cotton and can be used to dye the whole fabric or screen-print a motif. The temperature at which the dye will react can be set at 28°C, 30°C or 32°C, however, the effect lasts for only approximately five to ten washes. Photo-chromic dyes are now used on many products, for example novelty garments such as T-shirts with screen-printed logos.

Reflective inks – consist of minute glass balls that are screen-printed on to fabric. The glass reflects any available light back to the onlooker making the fabric highly visible in the dark and even reflective under water. The fabrics are also washable. A good example of clothing using these inks is the type worn by the emergency services.

Phosphorescent dyes – are smart dyes that can either be screen-printed or woven into fabric. They react to ultraviolet light making them appear to glow in the dark and highly visible. The dyes are non-toxic, colour-fast and washable. Products featuring them include protective clothing and novelty items such as jeans, T-shirts and tops with eye-catching prints and patterns.

Materials that release beneficial substances

Microscopic capsules containing beneficial substances such as vitamins, oils, antiseptics, aromatics, moisturisers or anti-bacterial agents can be incorporated into fabrics and yarns in a process called **micro-encapsulation**. The substances are then released by the gradual **abrasion** of the fabric by the skin.

Aromatic textiles are a particular growth area. They are scented to give off a pleasant aroma when the surface of the product is rubbed. Novelty items such as T-shirts with screen-printed images may give off a smell such as chocolate. The effects are quite long lasting and garments can be washed as normal. There are many other examples of the use of micro-encapsulation.

Underwear – fabrics are scented with the smell of different fruits, lavender and other calming scents and moisturising oils, or for men's underwear, aromas such as musk and sandalwood.

Medical products – wound dressings, bandages and medical stitches are encapsulated with antiseptic and medical and hospital garments are treated to absorb moisture.

Children's wear – for example, vests for children with sensitive skins are encapsulated with moisturisers and oils, and swimwear is encapsulated with sun block to prevent sunburn.

Sportswear – socks and sports clothing is treated to repel odour and fungal infections.

Household textiles – bed linen is encapsulated to smell of lavender and camomile and to aid relaxation and induce sleep.

Key words

Photo-chromic dyes change colour in response to a particular temperature.

Reflective inks reflect any available light making a garment more visible in the dark.

Phosphorescent dyes appear to glow in the dark.

Key words

Micro-encapsulation is the application of microscopic capsules to either a yarn or the surface of a fabric.

Abrasion is the scraping or wearing away of something.

Interactive textiles

These textiles involve the integration of conductive fibres such as carbon, silver and steel, and microchips into the fabric. As little as ten percent of the conductive fibre can be mixed with traditional fibres to give the fabric the conductivity to enable interaction with the user.

Conductive inks have also been developed which can be used to print a pattern on to fabric, which can then be electronically activated. There is a wide variety of potential applications for this technology, including the following.

Clothing – incorporating cameras is currently being developed that could help parents keep track of their children using technology such as global positioning satellites.

Levi's ICD – this jacket was developed by Levi's and Philips and incorporates a music and phone communications system accessed by headphones and built-in control.

Industrial applications – garments incorporating voice-activated computers which would leave workers' hands free to do other tasks.

Medical applications – headgear for paramedic incorporating tiny cameras to send visual information directly to the hospital so that a doctor can respond with immediate advice.

Entertainment – clothing that reacts to heat, lights and music.

Sportswear – that records activities, monitors progress and analyses performance while playing mood-enhancing music.

Automotive and transport industries – are the largest growth areas for technical and interactive textiles. They are used, for example, in clothing for car racing and motor biking, for space suits, in aircraft and space shuttles, and for automatic heated seats, seatbelts and airbags in cars.

Geotextiles

These fabrics can be bonded or woven from both synthetic and natural fibres. They have been used primarily in road construction and maintenance over the last twenty years. Examples from different industries include:

Fishing – aurora luminous nets that glow in the dark and increase night catches.

Construction – textile roofs, such as the Eden project in Cornwall and the Space Centre in Leicester.

Waterways – watertight geo-membranes used as canal liners stop water draining away.

Transport – geo textiles act as a layer of protection extending the life of the road or pavement.

Drainage and erosion – geo-membranes act as a filter allowing the passage of water and helping to control erosion and drainage.

> ### Key word
> **Interactive textiles** are touch- and pressure-sensitive fabrics incorporating conductive fibres.

> ### Key word
> **Geotextiles** are bonded or woven man-made and natural fabrics that can be made from polypropelene fibres.

Further development of smart and modern materials

It is important that you keep your knowledge up-to-date and that you are aware of new smart and modern materials as they become commercially available.

Key points

- You should be able to describe what is meant by the term 'smart material'.
- You should be able to give examples of the different types of smart materials available today.

Activity

Smart and modern materials will continue to change and develop rapidly. Use the Internet to access websites such as www.softswitch.co.uk and www.electrotextiles.com to collect details and compile a notebook of up-to-date developments and products.

Questions

1 Name and describe three smart and modern materials that are available today.

2 Describe three factors that cause smart dyes to change colour.

3 Give the performance characteristics of phosphorescence dyes.

4 Explain what micro-encapsulation is and give an example of a product that uses it.

5 Sportswear uses many types of smart and modern materials. Describe as many examples as you can.

Systems and control

This section will cover:

- Basic features of a control system
- Using systems and control in the textiles industry
- Regulating a system
- ICT-based management systems.

Basic features of a control system

There are three main types of control **system**: open loop, closed loop and large systems.

Open loop system

This is a simple system which gives no feedback information.

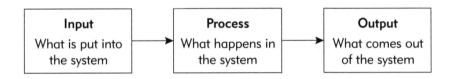

Closed loop system

This is a system that incorporates the feedback of information, which makes a system work well and enables a manufacturer to plan production and manufacture goods to order. Block diagrams like the one below are used to design and link systems and sub-systems that will produce different kinds of output.

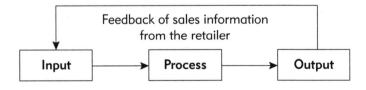

Large systems

These systems are made up of smaller sub-systems such as product design, assembly, finishing, packaging, stock control, and sales and marketing. The sub-systems can be linked together to work as a whole, by using product data management (PDM) or computer-integrated manufacture (CIM) software.

> **Key word**
>
> **A system** is a co-ordinated arrangement of activities in which inputs are processed to achieve outputs.

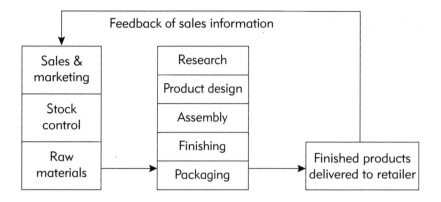

Using systems and control in the textiles industry

Different types of **system and control** are used to monitor the whole manufacturing process to ensure that textile products are manufactured efficiently at a profit. Control systems can be electrical, electronic, mechanical or computer-controlled. They can be used to regulate the many functions in a manufacturing business.

Regulating a system

Systems are regulated to ensure that items are assembled correctly. For example, the system to embroider a motif on a textile product must be checked and regulated to ensure that the machinery is consistently and correctly aligned to stitch the motif in the same place every time.

ICT-based management systems

There is a variety of ICT-based management systems:

Just in time (JIT) systems – make use of ICT to help plan the ordering of materials and components so they arrive at the factory just in time for production. They are complex systems that require careful planning between the manufacturer and supplier.

Stock control systems – are used to regulate the movement of fabrics and components around a factory so they are in the right place at the right time and also to continually assess retailers' stock supplies so that more stock can be ordered as needed to respond to customer demand.

Key points

- A control system has three elements: input, process and output.
- There are three main types of system: open loop, closed loop and large systems.
- There is usually a question on some aspect of systems and control in the examination.

Questions

1　Name and explain the three elements of a control system.

2　What is the advantage for a manufacturer of a closed loop system?

3　What does PDM stand for?

4　What is 'Just in time'?

Products and applications

This section will cover:

- Product analysis of commercially manufactured products and their applications.

Product analysis

In order to carry out the product analysis of a commercially manufactured product, you will need to take the following points into consideration.

- **Function and application** – establishing the intended function of the product, what it is meant to do and how it will be used.
- **The parts** – identifying the parts and their functions.
- **The way it works** – establishing how the product works and any scientific principles involved.
- **Materials** – identifying the materials the product is made of.
- **Manufacturing processes** – identifying which processes have been used to make the product.
- **Intended market** – establishing who or what is the intended market for the product.
- **Product performance** – assessing how well the product will work in comparison to alternative products or design solutions.
- **Testing** – using a variety of relevant tests.

One of the best ways to analyse and evaluate an existing textile product is to 'take it apart' to see how it has been made, including what materials, components and construction techniques have been used to make it. This process is known as disassembly. You could use a table like the one below to help you do this.

Product	Baseball cap
Function	Suggest reasons why people wear baseball caps.
Identification of parts	Including what type of fastening is used.
Materials	What fibres and fabrics are used? Do the materials have a special function – are they waterproof or washable? Why is this important?
Processes	How is the cap stitched together? What type of seam has been used? What manufacturing processes have been used?
Intended market	What type of person is the cap aimed at?
Performance	How successful is the style of the cap? List what you like and do not like about it. Is the price of the cap appropriate?
Testing	Compare this cap to a similar product. Carry out any relevant tests, for example waterproof test.

Quality

- Quality control
- Quality of design
- Quality of manufacture
- Care requirements
- Social, moral, economic, environmental and aesthetic issues.

Quality control

Quality control tests monitor the manufacture of textile products, checking that they all meet the relevant standards set for a well-made and safe product, which will help ensure that consumer and environmental expectations are also met. Materials, methods and inspection processes will be tested and particularly:

- raw materials and components for faults, fibre content, performance, wear, shrinkage and after-care
- match to design specifications including construction method, seam types, seam allowances, finishing, fabric, components and colour
- the final product, including comparing the size, fit and look of the product with a high quality prototype.

> ### Key word
> **Quality control** is a set of tests or inspections to ensure the manufacture of identical fault-free products, which meet all the standards set.

Quality of design

A product can be well-designed even if it is poorly made.

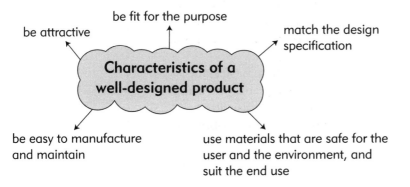

be fit for the purpose

be attractive

match the design specification

Characteristics of a well-designed product

be easy to manufacture and maintain

use materials that are safe for the user and the environment, and suit the end use

On the other hand, a badly-designed product, such as a baby bag that does not hold nappies, may not sell even if it is well-made and attractive.

Quality of manufacture

A product can be well-made even if it is poorly designed.

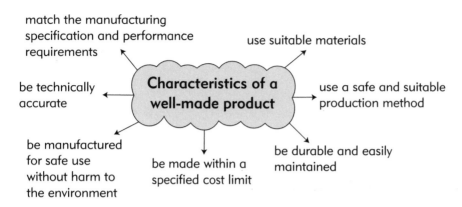

A badly-made baby bag that falls apart after three weeks may look good when it is new, but its poor reputation would limit future sales.

Care requirements

Care requirements are indicated by recognised symbols. You will need to know the standards and symbols that represent quality. The British Standard 5750 UK National Standards for Quality Systems introduced a scheme to ensure quality assurance. If a product passes the set requirements (see *GCSE Textiles Technology for OCR*, page 124) the BS 5750 (CEN 2900) provides a Firm Mark for operating an efficient 'Quality System'. Any company that is registered will have the BSI Firm Symbol (ISO 9000).

Social, moral, economic, environmental and aesthetic issues

The choices involved in deciding on the appropriate resources and materials to use in the production of textile products all have social, moral, economic, environmental and/or aesthetic implications. In particular, both design and manufacturing decisions and processes will have an impact on the type of materials and components used and the ways in which they are disposed of or recycled.

Improvements in manufacturing processes will help to protect the customer and preserve the environment. Man-made materials are made of disposable and biodegradable chemicals. Textile products can also be recycled, not just by passing down clothing, but by shredding fabrics and making new ones.

Key points

The key factors which help in making judgements about the quality of a product are:

- quality of design
- quality of manufacture
- appropriate use of materials and resources with regard to social, moral, economic, environmental and aesthetic issues.

Activity

Social, moral, economic, environmental and aesthetic implications are just some of the quality issues that need to be considered in the manufacture of textile products. Choose a product such as a bag and write a specification to show that you understand the difference between quality of design and quality of manufacture. In particular, refer to:

- the target market group
- non-toxic materials that are safe for the environment
- ease of manufacture
- design suitability and safety for the user and the environment.

Health and safety

This section will cover:

- Health and safety issues for designers
- Health and safety in the workplace
- Risk assessment
- Environmental factors.

Health and safety issues for designers

Product designers need to be aware of a wide range of health and safety issues, and must:

- take responsibility for the appropriate selection of materials and finishes

- use all available information to help assess any health and safety risks involved in the design, manufacture and end use of textile products.

Health and safety in the workplace

The Health and Safety at Work Act was introduced in 1974 and employers are legally responsible for the health and safety of their employees, who in turn are responsible to using the safety equipment provided. Here are some simple issues that could affect health and safety in the workplace:

The kite mark identifies products that have passed rigorous safety checks

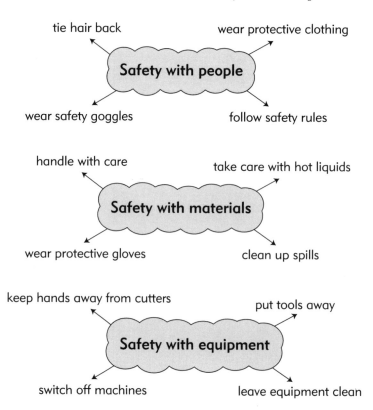

tie hair back

wear protective clothing

Safety with people

wear safety goggles

follow safety rules

handle with care

take care with hot liquids

Safety with materials

wear protective gloves

clean up spills

keep hands away from cutters

put tools away

Safety with equipment

switch off machines

leave equipment clean

There are many potential hazards in a production environment, but the following are the most important issues.

Ventilation – there must be adequate ventilation to protect those working with processes that cause dust or fumes, such as screen printing with dyes. Extractor fans and/or fume cupboards should be provided as appropriate.

Protective clothing – such as suitable goggles, masks, gloves, footwear, hard hat and overalls must be worn by some workers, for example those working with dyes and other chemicals.

Machine guards – are used to prevent injury, most usually to fingers and hands. The guards and suitable procedures must be in place to reduce the risk of accidents with machinery, such as sewing machines, or with hot steam, such as steam presses.

Accident and evacuation procedures – these must be displayed and give instruction on what to do in the case of an accident or a fire.

Storage of chemicals – must be stored according to the Control of Substances Hazardous to Health Regulations (COSHH) introduced in 1994. The regulations detail how each particular hazardous substance is to be stored and handled, and the procedures in case of accident. Substances must be kept in their original containers with instructions on how to use them and with the recognised warning labels displayed.

Risk assessment

All aspects of the workplace and the activities that take place there must be assessed for the risks involved, which must then be minimised. In the examination, you will need to be able to recognise and understand the warning labels and safety symbols shown in this section.
The British Standards Institute set standards to ensure that manufacturers fulfil the health and safety requirements.

Environmental factors

The textiles industry can have a direct impact on the environment, so environmental and cultural issues have to be taken into account when making decisions about the structure and function of the textiles and other materials used. There are two key areas to be considered.

Disposal of chemicals

The replacing of traditionally-used chemicals with natural substances or at least with biodegradable chemicals used wherever possible is a major issue. The chemicals that are used must be efficiently removed from water supplies. Recycling water, chemicals and/or energy is also desirable.

Recycling

Concern for the environment has also impacted on the recycling of yarns, fabrics and clothing. For example, plastic bottles can be recycled to produce fibres to make polartec fleece, reducing the need to use new materials and the waste destined for a landfill site or incinerator.

The Eco-tex Standard 100 label may be used on products that contain no harmful substances and that have been made with the minimum damage to the environment. The European eco-label is based on the vision of 'greening non-food products all over Europe'. This may have an impact on the cost of the products.

The European eco-label

European Eco-label

Key points

- Safety needs to be designed into a product, e.g. nightwear should be fire retardant, toys for children aged under 36 months should not have small parts.
- Employers and employees have responsibilities to ensure health and safety in the workplace.
- All risks must be assessed and minimised.
- Companies and consumers are becoming increasingly conscious of environmental issues.

Activities

1 Find out about the health and safety rules in your textiles area at school.
2 Research other examples of eco-labels you can find.
3 Compare the cost of similar products with and without the eco-label.

Specimen exam questions

One full foundation paper and one full higher tier paper are given on the following pages. The mark schemes, showing the full marks available for each question, are given after the sample papers.

Key points

- All full course candidates take two examination papers.
- Higher candidates working towards Grades A* to D take Papers 2 and 4, each lasting one hour and fifteen minutes.
- Foundation candidates working towards Grades C to G take Papers 1 and 3, each lasting one hour.
- Each paper has five tiered questions, each worth ten marks.
- All the questions will be based on textiles technology.
- The questions will require a mixture of written, sketched and annotated answers.

Sample questions

Foundation tier paper

1a Complete the chart below. Name a different *fibre* or *fabric* that could be used to make each item.

Item	Fibre or fabric
Cushion	Silk
Duvet cover	
Blanket	
Tablecloth	

(3)

1b Give a reason for your choice of fibre or fabric for each item.

Duvet (1)

_____

Blanket (1)

_____

Tablecloth (1)

_____

1c Suggest *four* suitable fastenings for either a cushion or a duvet. (4)

_____

_____

_____

_____

2a The symbols below were found on a care label on a duvet cover made from poly-cotton. Explain what each symbol means. (3)

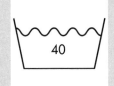

_____   _____   _____

2b The duvet cover was sewn using an overlocker to finish the edges. Suggest two *advantages* and two *disadvantages* of an overlocker. (4)

_____

_____

_____

_____

2c Name *three* surface decoration techniques to add pattern to the duvet cover. (3)

_____

_____

_____

3a A designer needs to choose a fabric to be used to make a child's bag. The fabric will need to have certain performance characteristics. Write down *three* performance characteristics of your chosen fabric. (3)

_____

_____

_____

3b A logo needs to be applied to your bag. Sketch your logo and state how you would apply it to your bag. (4)

3c The bag needs to be fastened securely. The components used should be safe for young children. Explain your choice of fastening and the reason why you have chosen it. (3)

_____

_____

4 The hooded waistcoat illustrated below is to be constructed in a school environment.

Lined

Hood

Zip

Nylon fabric

Velcro pocket

a Write a specification for the hooded waistcoat. (4)

_____

_____

_____

_____

b Explain how CAD and CAM would be used to ensure efficient working practice in the design and cutting of the fabric pieces. (2)

_____

_____

c Pattern symbols need to be drawn on the pattern pieces. Draw the symbols for:

Grain line

Notches/balance marks

Lay on folded edge of fabric (3)

d Name a suitable method of manufacture for 50 to be made. (1)

_____

5a A sports company wishes to manufacture a fleece top for teenagers. Modify the existing design below to take account of the following specification points.

Attractiveness

Fastenings

Additional features

Annotate your design ideas. (6)

5b Give reasons why including these specification points in their new sports range will increase sales of the fleece tops. (4)

_____

_____

_____

_____

Higher tier paper

1a The specification below is for a rucksack which is to be made from a canvas fabric. Complete the specification by adding *three* design features for the bag. (3)

- Must be easy to carry and leave the hands free.

- Must have a detachable purse.

- _____

- _____

- _____

1b A prototype will be made by the manufacturer. What is a prototype? (2)

_____

_____

1c The manufacturer has decided to use a striped fabric. What factors should you consider before producing designs in striped fabric? (3)

_____

_____

_____

1d Small valuable items are stored in the detachable purse. Suggest a suitable method of attaching this purse to the main part of the bag. (2)

_____

_____

2a Sketch a design for a cushion to be used on a chair in a reception area. Annotate your ideas to show you have taken into account the following specification points:

Attractiveness

Additional features such as fastenings

Fabric finishes (6)

2b What are the advantages of using CAD (computer-aided design) to develop the cushion design?

(4

_____

_____

_____

_____

3 A wall hanging is required to co-ordinate with the cushions. The wall hanging will have an appliquéd motif.

a List the *five* main stages in the preparation and machine stitching of the motif on to the wall hanging.

(5)

_____

_____

_____

_____

_____

b Name an alternative method of producing a pattern on the wall hanging.

(1)

_____

c The edges of the wall hanging are to be overlocked. Give *two* advantages and *two* disadvantages of overlocking.

(4)

_____   _____

_____   _____

4a Industrial patterns could be used for commercial production. Explain how the manufacturer could use information technology when designing the pattern pieces.

(3)

_____

_____

4b Patterns used for commercial production are different to those used to make a 'one-off' or a prototype. Identify *three* features of an industrial pattern and explain how they would be used. (3)

_____

_____

_____

4c What are the advantages of using information technology to develop the cutting plan? (4)

_____

_____

_____

_____

5a Health and safety in the workplace is essential to manufacturers. Explain *five* implications for a manufacturer when health and safety is neglected. (5)

_____

_____

_____

_____

_____

5b Care of the environment has become an increasing concern for consumers. Explain how the textiles industry is responding to this concern. (5)

_____

_____

_____

_____

_____

Answers to questions

Foundation tier paper

1a Answer can be any suitable fibre or fabric but no repeats.

    Duvet: cotton, cotton polyester, cotton lawn, denim. (1)
    Blanket: wool, fleece, acrylic, and polyester. (1)
    Tablecloth: linen, PVC, lace, silk, nylon, viscose. (1)

1b No repeats for answer.

    Duvet: easy to wash, soft, durable, not too expensive. (1)
    Blanket: warmth, comfort, length of life, washable soft, cost. (1)
    Tablecloth: hygiene, easy to clean, appearance, cost, non-absorbent. (1)

1c Answer can be any four different fastenings from the list below:

    Zip, button, popper, tie, toggle, Velcro, hook & eye. (4)

2a Temperature to use to avoid damage.

    Machine washable at 40°C. (1)
    Can be tumble dried/tumble dry. (1)
    Iron on a warm setting/160°C. (1)

2b Two of each of the following.

    Advantages: neatens the edges, stops fraying, neat professional finish, quicker as it sews and neatens in one. (2)
    Disadvantages: limited use, difficult to thread, expensive for threads/needs more thread, higher maintenance costs, mistakes are more difficult to correct. (2)

2c Any three surface techniques from the list below.

    Hand stitching, beading, quilting, appliqué, machine embroidery, screen-printing. (2)

3a Choice of fabric should relate to the fibre content and performance characteristics of the fabric such as the following.

    Easy care, washability, hard-wearing, strength, texture, resistance to staining, safety issues. (3)

3b Two marks awarded for the suitability of sketched logo and the detail such as colour and pattern in which it is done. (2)

    Two marks awarded for a relevant method of application, for example screen-printing, POEM embroidery machine, CAD, with a description or reason for choice. (2)

3c One mark for the choice of fastening. (1)

    Two marks for the reason for choice and suitability for a child, with reference to safety and ease of fastening. (2)

4a Four marks awarded for relevant specification points, for example:

Hood: to keep your head warm and dry, protection from the wind.
Zip fastening: to keep warm, ease of use, unisex feature.
Nylon fabric: lightweight, strong, quick drying, water resistant.
Lining: extra warmth.
Velcro pockets: store equipment securely. (4)

4b Two marks for any of the following points:

CAD: ease of changing design and colour, increase or decrease sizes, help with pattern lay, economical use of fabric, reduces waste.
CAM: cut multiple layers of fabric at the same time, reduces production time (2)

4c One mark for each correctly drawn symbol:

Straight of grain/grain line. (1)

Notches/ balance marks. (1)

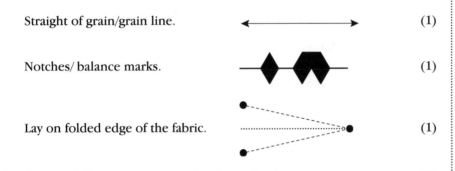

Lay on folded edge of the fabric. (1)

4d One mark for correct answer: batch production. (1)

5a Two marks for each any of the following design features.

Attractiveness: braid, colour, use of contrasting colour indicated or shown, logo, design, type of fleece.
Fastenings: for example zip, toggle, buttons and loops, Velcro, drawstring.
Additional features: for example drawstring, cord, pockets, elastic cuff, 3D effect, quilting, embroidery, hood, attached gloves. (6)

5b Four marks for the explanation, referring to the following points: opens up the range to more people, either sex or unisex, more customer appeal, suitable for more occasions. (4)

Higher tier paper

1a Answers can be any three of the following:

Pockets: zipped compartments, any mention of relevant fastening.
Adjustable straps.
Waterproof material.
Strong handles. (3)

1b A prototype is a one-off or model to test out what the actual one would look like. (2)

1c Answers can be any three of the following:

Effects created from stripes: can look taller/thinner.
Creative patterns: cut pieces with stripes running in different directions or with stripes on the cross.
More fabric will be needed to match, which may add to the cost of the product.
Stripes need to be balanced on the item: centred/at corners.
The look of the overall effect.
Consideration of the size of the stripe. (3)

1d Any suitable fastening with a reason for choice, for example:

Zip: secure and safe.
Velcro: quick and effective to use. (2)

2a For the suitability of the sketched cushion and the detail in which it is done, including for example colour, pattern size, measurements or shape. (2)

For additional features such as:
Fastenings: zip, buttons, ties, toggles, Velcro.
Suggested technique for decoration such as appliqué, embroidery, quilting, frill, piping, or lace, or ribbon, tassels/braid. (2)
For reference to two fabric finishes: stain resistant, colour-fast, flame retardent, fire retardent, resistant to light fading. (2)

2b For any of the following points:

Try/experiment and store different ideas.
Adapt easily/reposition/deleting.
Store to develop later.
Lay planning.
Try colour ways.
Can reverse/mirror ideas.
View it from different angles/or 3D.
Re-proportion /change size.
Accuracy/quality/professional.
Make template of cushion patterns.
Can download ideas directly to manufacturing machinery, for example POEM or cutter/heat transfer. (4)

3a Any five points in logical order:

Make pattern/template/stencil.
Use Vilene/Bondaweb.
Cut fabric.
Pin/tack in place/use of Bondaweb (iron).
Machine with a zigzag stitch/sew it on.
Press/trim ends. (5)

3b For any alternative method: screen-printing, transfer printing, batik, quilting, embroidery. (1)

3c For any two of the following advantages and for any two of the following disadvantages:

Advantages:

- neatens the edges/stops fraying
- quicker, sews and neatens in one operation
- neat professional finish. (2)

Disadvantages:

- more expensive maintenance costs
- expensive for threads
- limited use
- can be difficult to thread

4a One mark for each correct point, three required.

Shapes could already be held in memory.
Shapes can be drawn on the screen and then stored.
Shapes can be scanned in and then stored.
Can be graded up or down in size.
Pattern markings can be added. (3)

4b One mark for each correct point, three required.

Pattern may not be used, may be a computer-generated image.
Cut and balance marks are different.
Pattern would be 'opened out'; there would be no place on fold.
The pattern would need to be laid on flat, unfolded fabric, so that layers could be built up.
Hundreds of layers of fabric could be cut in industry without folds.
This saves time, therefore money. (3)

4c One mark for each correct point, four required.

Most economical cutting plan can be devised and stored.
Shapes can easily be manipulated on screen and experimented with.
Different widths of fabric can be tried.
Shows which pieces need to be cut twice or reversed.
Accurate and avoids mistakes.
Can download directly to the cutting machine.
Costs can be calculated. (4)

5a One mark for each correct answer with an explanation, five required.

Low staff morale.
Bad reputation.
Loss of profit.
Fines levied.
Legal action.
Compensation sought.
Inefficiency of product and quality of product. (5)

5b One mark for each correct answer with an explanation, five required.

Recycling waste fabric and waste chemicals.
Supplier or waste disposal company contracted to remove legally.
Natural fibres – plants and animals managed carefully – minimal damage to the environment.
Use of natural fibres – biodegradable.
Use of recycled plastic for new synthetic fibres.
Transportation of raw materials kept to a minimum – prevent pollution by producing goods near to raw material sites.
Use of modern vehicles to reduce emissions.
Insulation of buildings.
Designing long lasting products – reduces repetitive production. (5)